Why Intranets Fail (and How to Fix Them)

CHANDOS
INFORMATION PROFESSIONAL SERIES

Series Editor: Ruth Rikowski
(email: rikowski@tiscali.co.uk)

Chandos' new series of books are aimed at the busy information professional. They have been specially commissioned to provide the reader with an authoritative view of current thinking. They are designed to provide easy-to-read and (most importantly) practical coverage of topics that are of interest to librarians and other information professionals. If you would like a full listing of current and forthcoming titles, please visit our web site **www.chandospublishing.com** or contact Hannah Grace-Williams on email info@chandospublishing.com or telephone number +44 (0) 1865 884447.

New authors: we are always pleased to receive ideas for new titles; if you would like to write a book for Chandos, please contact Dr Glyn Jones on email gjones@chandospublishing.com or telephone number +44 (0) 1865 884447.

Bulk orders: some organisations buy a number of copies of our books. If you are interested in doing this, we would be pleased to discuss a discount. Please contact Hannah Grace-Williams on email info@chandospublishing.com or telephone number +44 (0) 1865 884447.

Why Intranets Fail
(and How to Fix Them)

*A practical guide for
information professionals*

LUKE TREDINNICK

Chandos Publishing
Oxford · England · New Hampshire · USA

Chandos Publishing (Oxford) Limited
Chandos House
5 & 6 Steadys Lane
Stanton Harcourt
Oxford OX29 5RL
UK
Tel: +44 (0) 1865 884447 Fax: +44 (0) 1865 884448
Email: info@chandospublishing.com
www.chandospublishing.com

Chandos Publishing USA
3 Front Street, Suite 331
PO Box 338
Rollinsford, NH 03869
USA
Tel: 603 749 9171 Fax: 603 749 6155
Email: BizBks@aol.com

First published in Great Britain in 2004

ISBN:
1 84334 068 2 (paperback)
1 84334 093 3 (hardback)

© L. Tredinnick, 2004

British Library Cataloguing-in-Publication Data.
A catalogue record for this book is available from the British Library.

All rights reserved. No part of this publication may be reproduced, stored in or introduced into a retrieval system, or transmitted, in any form, or by any means (electronic, mechanical, photocopying, recording or otherwise) without the prior written permission of the Publishers. This publication may not be lent, resold, hired out or otherwise disposed of by way of trade in any form of binding or cover other than that in which it is published without the prior consent of the Publishers. Any person who does any unauthorised act in relation to this publication may be liable to criminal prosecution and civil claims for damages.

The Publishers make no representation, express or implied, with regard to the accuracy of the information contained in this publication and cannot accept any legal responsibility or liability for any errors or omissions.

The material contained in this publication constitutes general guidelines only and does not represent to be advice on any particular matter. No reader or purchaser should act on the basis of material contained in this publication without first taking professional advice appropriate to their particular circumstances.

Cover images courtesy of Bytec Solutions Ltd (*www.bytecweb.com*) and David Hibberd (*DAHibberd@aol.com*).

Contents

Acknowledgements

I would like to thank Julie Fowler and Amy Page, who both contributed in many small ways over many years to the ideas that formulated this book. I would also like to thank the staff and students at the Information Management School, London Metropolitan University. Lastly, I would like to thank Elizabeth, just because.

List of tables and figures

List of tables

List of figures

Introduction

The trouble with intranets

Information is a troublesome thing: there is never so much of it as when you know exactly what you need; never so little as when you do not. Information professionals are destined to walk this fine line between too much information and too little. Just enough is almost never the right amount.

Bradford's law of scatter implies that 80 per cent of the demand on any collection will be satisfied by 20 per cent of that collection (Bradford, 1934). There are always the key reference texts you turn to time and again, the dependable websites at the top of your favourites list, the same questions asked every day. Yet it is the 20 per cent of more taxing information demands that cause all the problems.

There should thus be nothing more logical and straightforward than shifting those heavily in demand resources to the users' desktops, thereby freeing an organisation to concentrate on the more troublesome information needs. An intranet, the theory suggests, will liberate the human resources department from answering the same frequently asked questions about holiday entitlements and sick-leave, enabling them to concentrate on their core business of recruitment and retention. It will allow the marketing department to market, rather than becoming trapped in distributing endless promotional material within the organisation. All the information that people most often ask of each other can be relegated to an intranet.

Once released from the dependence on interpersonal communicative processes for its dissemination, this most-in-demand information, the lifeblood and intellectual capital of any organisation, should flow more easily. Employees should no longer be left to leaf through an internal directory pondering just where to go for information because *it's on the intranet*. This phrase echoes around the corridors of the corporate world:

Where can I ... ?

It's on the intranet!

What do I ... ?

It's on the intranet!

Who am I ... ?

It's on the intranet!

And in this idealised organisation machine the intranet functions like a reservoir that feeds the oil of information to smooth the turning of the cogs that make the whole thing work.

So, why does it not work like that?

Why do intranets frequently become a burden: resource-heavy, and so very difficult to use? Why do they fail to deliver what was expected of them five years ago? Did we expect too much, or did something go wrong along the way?

A new world brain

When Tim Berners-Lee formulated the specifications for HTML and the World Wide Web (hereafter the Web) in the late 1980s, he drew no distinction between information housed locally and that housed at a distance. In his view, whether a file was located on the desktop computer, on another computer in the organisation or halfway around the world should not influence the mechanisms by which the user approached obtaining it. What really mattered to the user, he thought, was how the information related to their needs. The Web was designed as one global information resource that would arrange *all* information by semantic and associative connections, regardless of its location. Those connections became encoded in HTML as the hyperlinks that we use to navigate the Web. They replaced traditional hierarchical approaches to ordering information with meaningful relationships based on association, mirroring the way people think (Berners-Lee, 1999).

It is for this reason that the first real use for the Web was what would now be considered an intranet application: an internal phone book. For Berners-Lee, the associations on which hypertext webs could be built within organisations were no different from the association on which hypertext webs could be built between organisations. The intranet and extranet were all a part of his vision for the Web.

However, the Web developed away from Berners-Lee's vision in two critical ways. Firstly, when they were initially developed, organisations were reluctant to allow unrestricted communication between intranets and the Internet. This resulted in intranets growing up as distinct and secure information resources – safe, mini-internets. For the user, whether information was held internally or externally became an issue with which they need concern themselves once again. Local and global information resources were divided, and the user had to approach each by different means.

Secondly, the tools of the Web developed in such a way as to separate the processes of creating and disseminating information. The Web is built around HTML. Two pieces of software are critical in this: editing packages that create the HTML pages, such as Dreamweaver or Microsoft Front-Page, and Internet browsers to view the pages, such as Netscape Navigator and Microsoft Explorer. Berners-Lee initially saw no distinction between the functions of creating and viewing HTML: the web browser should also be the web editor. Anybody with the right permission should be able to view a page through their browser, and if necessary to alter it – add a hyperlink, correct errors, etc. In this way, web pages were intended as shared resources, created by collaboration between any number of individuals to whom the owner of the resource had given access and editing permissions. These ideas were not fully implemented by software developers. Perhaps Tim Berners-Lee's vision was too much like an *intra*net and too little like an *inter*net.

The Web works as a business tool in which intranets fail because on the whole people *communicate* with those from other organisations, but they *collaborate* with those from their own. To date, browser technology prioritises the communicative function above the collaborative. It has not allowed collaboration to take place seamlessly. It still matters whether information is housed locally or at a distance.

How to use this book

This book argues that intranets can deliver real benefits in information management and organisational efficiency, and that the best intranets do exactly that, but that in order to achieve these goals we need to readdress the problem of failing intranets and identify why they fall short of their full potential.

It will not tell you how to set up web servers or mark up pages in HTML, how to use Dreamweaver, HotMetal or FrontPage, select a content management system or design your pages to match a corporate identity. There are already many other books that can explain all these things perfectly adequately. This book is concerned with information architecture: about organising intranets in the most effective and efficient way. It is about the vagaries of organisational behaviour: about why organisations operate in a way that very often frustrates principles of good information management. Most importantly, it is a book about people: about the ways in which people interact with intranets in their workspaces or study-spaces, about why they behave in what can sometimes appear to be an irrational way. By the very simplest definition, intranets are just a way of getting information to people. In order that they do so effectively, we need to understand how people behave.

The first half of this book examines users and organisations, and their influence on intranet management. Chapter 1 examines user behaviour, and explains why users behave in a way that is unanticipated. Chapter 2 focuses on organisational structures and examines how large organisations function within the context of intranet management. Chapter 3 explains how the competing expectations of both the organisation and the user can be reconciled. The second half of the book explains how to organise, design and manage intranets within this user- and organisation-orientated approach. Information architecture and intranet design are covered in Chapter 4, the process of implementing and managing intranets in Chapters 5 and 6, and future directions in Chapter 7.

The advice in this book is intended for the organisation and management of entire intranets, although it will hold true for sections of intranets, particularly self-contained sections with distinct resources such as library or information services sites. Each chapter can be treated as a self-contained unit. However, the book builds into a developed argument, and it is advisable to read through the book sequentially at least once.

About the author

Luke Tredinnick currently works as a Senior Lecturer in Information Management at London Metropolitan University. He previously worked as a Systems Librarian and Intranet Content Manager for a large financial services firm. He specialises in all aspects of managing information in the digital environment.

The author may be contacted as follows:

Luke Tredinnick
London Metropolitan University
Department of Applied Social Sciences
Ladbroke House
62–66 Highbury Grove
London N5 2AD

E-mail: *l.tredinnick@londonmet.ac.uk*

Part 1
Failing intranets

Failing intranets?

It is not difficult to find evidence of failing intranets. *Information World Review*'s headline in June 2001, 'Intranets Failing', echoed the prevailing interpretation of a survey by US research and advisory service, Outsell, into knowledge workers' views of external content within their workplaces. The article branded intranets a 'dismal failure', citing poor search-engine capabilities and static content as the cause of user dissatisfaction (Information World Review, 2001).

This interpretation can hardly have come as a surprise to an industry that had struggled from the outset to realise the true business benefits of intranets. Two years before the Outsell research, Cranfield University suggested not only that large corporate intranets were failing to deliver real value, but also that public-sector intranets languished in a state of under-development (August, 1999). Martin White has pointed to a UK House of Commons select committee report indicating that the overall effectiveness of intranets in central government is poor (White, 2002). More recently, Mercer (2003) concluded that company intranets can be a waste of time, being treated as dumping-grounds for information of limited value that has no other home, and failing to reflect an overall corporate communications strategy. Figures from Keynote Market Reports (2004) reveal that intranet penetration *declined* between 2001 and 2002, citing the Mercer research as a possible explanation.

The cost of failing intranets

But what is the cost of this failure?

Initially there are the resources consumed in the development of an intranet, including hardware and software costs, licensing costs and most significantly staff time. But there are further indirect costs of failing intranets: the loss of productivity caused by staff failing to find information, finding the wrong information or finding the right information but spending an inordinate amount of time in doing so. In his book, *Designing Web Usability*, Jakob Nielsen estimated that one badly written news headline on a company's main intranet page read by 10,000 employees could cost $5,000 in lost productivity (Nielsen, 2000). The cost of failing intranets is great indeed.

Intranets are predominantly budgeted for in terms of the tangible costs in providing the service. This may include the hardware and software costs, licensing costs, staff time in developing content and time spent in managing the intranet. These costs may be set against an often arbitrary figure to represent the increases in efficiency that the intranet is intended to introduce. But intranets only achieve these efficiency gains if they are used as a primary information resource. If half of an organisation's personnel use paper-based procedures manuals and half use intranet-based manuals, the duplication of effort in providing the two resources results in a proportional reduction in efficiency savings.

The solution is to make one or other the only available version: to force users into a single medium (Blackmore, 2001). But it is not quite as straightforward as this. People have varying IT skills levels: some are more comfortable with intranet technology than others. This creates a patchwork of efficiency gain and loss. Although the production process is undoubtedly cheaper, some users spend more time than previously accessing information. Zipf (1949) predicted that most people, most of the time, are deterred by small hurdles, and that for behaviour to become habitual, it needs to be almost effortless. Users presented with a potential increase in effort may find alternative means to fulfil their information requirements. Common strategies include printing and keeping intranet content in paper form, dispelling any hopes that an intranet aids control over version management.

The effect of a poorly implemented intranet, therefore, is to shift costs from the central processing and ordering of information and spread those costs across individual employees. It may appear that the organisation is saving money, because printing and distribution costs have reduced, but at the same time hidden costs have been added. An intranet that does not bear down on its costs will fail to bring business benefits, even if it succeeds as an information resource. That means that managing the costs of intranets in comparison with other information resources is just as important as managing the cost of maintaining the intranet.

Why intranets fail

Having grown organically from a small beginning, many corporate intranets become steadily more inconsistent and out of date as they develop (Robertson, 2002b). The larger an unmanaged intranet becomes, the harder it will be for users to access information, because there is little underlying logic or structure for them to follow. Reports on usability testing by the Usability Company (Neal, 2002) suggested that many organisations launch intranets without the right preparation, and Flood (2001a) cites evidence that corporate intranets often fail because of a lack of understanding of end-user needs. Coulson-Thomas (2001) has argued that IT specialists tend to concentrate upon issues relating to data and information rather than usability, and that too often the capture and storage of information is perceived as an end in itself. Often, no consideration has been given to any later extraction of that information.

Robertson (2002b) identified key signs of languishing intranets, including:

- low and static staff usage;
- a majority of out-of-date, incomplete or inaccurate content;
- inconsistency of appearance;
- few or no controls over what can be published;
- content review and other editorial procedures limited or non-existent;
- a lack of clearly defined business goals for the intranet.

Evident from the above studies is not only the lack of any real progress towards the acceptance of intranets as a tool delivering real business benefit, but also the consistency of the charges laid against failing intranets. Time and again the same issues are raised: poor search performance, poor navigation structure, out-of-date and static content, users failing to find relevant information or, worse still, abandoning intranets for more pervasive information resources such as the Web.

Are we to imagine, then, that intranet managers have failed to make any progress towards successful information architecture in the last few years, that they have learned nothing from the experiences of web design? Some years ago the Web was mired under similar usability issues, but the Web matured and designers learned from collective experience. Why do intranets suffer a similar set of basic problems relating to usability year after year?

Some of the answers are no doubt in the inherently secret nature of intranets: organisations are reluctant to share their endeavours with others, and therefore every stage of good design has to be reinvented with every new intranet project. However, a growing literature over several years has failed to impact on the generally poor perception of intranets.

It was not meant to be like this. An intranet was meant to be the key to tapping the unrealised resource of an organisation's own intellectual capital, unlocking hidden business potential. The second-hand, often inaccurate and sometimes deliberately deceitful or scurrilous information that makes up the Web should not be perceived to be of more value to an organisation than its own intellectual capital. The technology is fundamentally the same, but the content of intranets *should* make them more critical to business success.

So why do intranets fail organisations when the Web works?

1

Why users behave irrationally

Aims

This chapter explores how people relate to intranets in their day-to-day work, and how usage impacts on intranet design and management. The chapter focuses on four key areas:

- user perspectives on intranets
- types of user
- user behaviour
- user expectations.

User perspectives on intranets

Repeated studies have revealed that users rate three factors as most important to the function of their organisation's intranet:

- an effective search engine
- good navigation aids
- up-to-date and relevant content.

In other words, users want to be able to locate information, and for that information to match their needs. A successful intranet must get these basics right. However, findings also suggest most users regard their intranets as only partially successful in these three areas. This gap between what users want from intranets and what they get results in the low levels of user satisfaction attributable to many intranets.

Competing perspectives

What do users mean when they express a desire for effective search engines, good navigation, and up-to-date and relevant content? Do intranets really fail at these basics, or do information and IT professionals understand different things by these concepts than users?

When users complain of poor search facilities, they are reflecting on their experience of searching the intranet and the results they achieve. They do not care necessarily what search engine has been deployed, how fully the intranet is indexed, whether deep-web pages in alternative or proprietary formats such as word processor documents or Adobe Acrobat documents have been included in the index, how the search engine weights results or whether there is an advanced search option available. They are simply expressing that when they type in a search term, they do not find what they are looking for.

However, when information professionals discuss search facilities, it is the technological aspects of search engines on which they focus. They are used to regarding search technology as a product of the comprehensiveness of the indexing combined with the effectiveness of the weighting and the presentation of results. When users say they cannot find information that matches their needs using the search engine, we respond not by exploring these needs, but by adjusting the tools they use to find it and exploring training issues.

Similarly, information professionals have a more sophisticated view of taxonomical navigation aids than users. When users complain that they cannot find information using the navigation aids, we respond by assessing the relationships between the terms that form the navigation structure, reflecting on the suitability of each as a descriptor, and deepening or flattening the hierarchy. But users do not approach navigation from this perspective. They are unlikely to have reflected on the relationships between the parts of a navigation scheme. What they understand by poor navigation is that they are failing to find what they started out looking for.

Again, information professionals may relate each item of content to the organisation's objectives and to a wider strategy for information provision via the intranet. Rigorous procedures may have been introduced to ensure that this content is up to date. This will in itself only marginally improve user perception. By irrelevant or out-of-date content, users do not necessarily mean that it is of no relevance to an organisation, or that it serves no needs, but that when they look for information, what they find is not relevant to their own needs *at that time*.

These three issues can be summarised thus: when users look for information either by searching or browsing, they are perhaps finding information that is like what they need, or perhaps information that is unlike what they need, but they are not finding exactly what they need with enough reliability to impact on their low levels of satisfaction. Although users identify search, navigation and content as the causes of their frustration, this is only because search, navigation and content are the components that they associate with using intranets. It does not necessarily follow that they are the causes of failing intranets.

Failing intranets or failing users?

Most intranets are equipped with adequate search engines. Most intranet navigation schemes are planned and logical. Most intranets have content management strategies in place. But intranets are still failing. This being the case, there can be only three possible reasons behind the three common complaints:

- The information on the intranet is organised sufficiently badly that neither searching nor browsing can guarantee its recovery.

- User-strategies for finding information are ineffective.

- The required information is simply not available.

The usual course is to blame the users once the navigation aids, search engines and provision of content have been determined to be adequate. This book suggests an alternative approach.

Making an intranet usable means enabling the user to get to the information they want with enough reliability to make them want to use that intranet as the primary resource for certain of their information needs. In order to do so, we must understand how the experience of using intranets creates a situation in which information becomes difficult to find. We must step outside our perspective as information professionals, who perhaps understand our intranets rather too well, and look from the point of view of the user, who neither knows our intranet well nor cares to find out.

Types of user

If users came shrink-wrapped with preset default settings like software, the world would be a less complicated place for intranet managers. Users of any system, however, vary greatly in their outlook and aptitudes. In order for that system to be sufficiently usable, it needs to be targeted simultaneously at a range of individual needs. This is of course impossible; that which best suits one user will not suit another.

Understanding user experiences requires that we first understand users. The broad behavioural patterns of each user will influence the effectiveness of their usage. For intranets, we can identify six broad groups:

- *Expert users* understand what the intranet is for, how it is structured, exactly what information it contains and how to obtain to that information. Just as importantly, they understand what the intranet does not contain. They will spend large amounts of time surveying the information terrain of the intranet and learning the layout of the content in detail. They will usually be heavily involved in the creation of content or the management of the intranet.

- *Skilled users* may have had some involvement in creating intranet content and therefore have had time to develop an understanding of the intranet. They will not know the entire intranet well, but they may know parts of it very well, and will be comfortable using navigational aids and search facilities to locate information, even within unfamiliar areas. They will have a good understanding of the types of information that are likely to be available on the intranet, and the types of information for which they are better turning to other resources.

- *Subject-orientated users* may or may not be involved with the production of the intranet. They understand those parts of the intranet they use frequently, such as departmental sites, in terms of both their scope and their content. However, they may only infrequently use parts of the intranet outside this limited area, possibly because previous attempts to do so have been frustrated.

■ *Process-junkies* learn the individual steps in any process without ever quite mastering the *purpose* of each of those steps. They may know, for example, that in order to print a document from Word they need to select File and then Print and then click on OK, but may be unable to print from another application. Process-junkies learn the processes for each task afresh in every new context, and may have lists of instructions for different tasks in different applications written down. They are easily thrown by novel tasks or by changing user environments.

■ *Intranet-shy users* may appear adept in their use of the World Wide Web and e-mail, to the extent that their lack of confidence around technology may go unnoticed. They will use the intranet when they have no other choice, particularly when directed to specific pages via well-signposted links to deep content. They may well venture into the search engine, and they may well follow a few links in the navigation aids, but whatever they do they will do tentatively, and quickly give up.

■ *Invisible users* will not use the intranet to find information no matter how essential it may be for them. They will get by with the conviction that the intranet is not for them, that it is unusable and not worth bothering with, a technological gimmick that has no role in their work or with any number of other excuses. They may rely on other resources for the information they need, such as paper resources or very often other people.

Expert and skilled users will always be in the minority within an organisation because the degree of exposure to an intranet required to become expert or skilled in using it is prohibitive. Quite how prohibitive will depend on the size and layout of the intranet, and therefore part of the function of intranet design is to minimise the influence of these factors. That said, relatively unskilled users will always form the majority user-group, for reasons that are developed later in this book.

User behaviour

The predominant characteristics of the user-groups discussed above will influence the use individuals make of an intranet. For example, subject-orientated users will stick with areas of content they know well, and process-junkies will stick with means of finding content that they understand.

We can categorise the ways users interact with intranets at any given time using qualities of that behaviour: the information-seeking strategy they adopt, either browsing, searching or targeting a known piece of information; their objectives, either concrete or limited; and their expectation of finding what they started out looking for. This produces the matrix represented in Table 1.1, which translates into five distinct categories of usage: speculative browsing; speculative searching; goals-orientated browsing; goals-orientated searching; and targeted information retrieval. Individual users may move between categories of usage, depending on their precise objectives at any given time.

It is important to note that these behaviour types are defined by user expectations, rather than by their technological approaches to finding information. For example:

- *Speculative browsing or searching.* Users will not have concrete goals or objectives in mind. They may be passing the time, or they may be surveying the information

Table 1.1   Factors in user behaviour

Strategy	Objectives	Expectation of content availability	Expectation of success	Behaviour type
Browsing	Unfixed	Low	Low	Speculative browsing
	Concrete	High	Mixed	Goals-orientated browsing
Searching	Unfixed	Low	Low	Speculative searching
	Concrete	High	Mixed	Goals-orientated Searching
Targeting	Concrete	High	High	Targeted information retrieval

terrain, but they have limited expectations about the information they might find. A typical example of this kind of behaviour is browsing or searching to ascertain the coverage available on a given topic of interest. Users will spend more time online when using an intranet speculatively than in other forms of usage.

- *Goals-orientated browsing or searching.* Users have in mind exactly what information they need and are attempting to find it systematically. They may do so by browsing likely locations or by searching. In either case they will have clear expectations about their likelihood of success or failure informing their use.

- *Targeted information retrieval.* Users know what information they are after and where it is, and they have a very high expectation of retrieving it. They may have the page bookmarked, or they may have used the particular resource enough times and know exactly how to find it. Usage of this kind is very brief in duration. Users retrieve the information without much conscious thought about the process they are going through and will normally put it to use immediately.

Defining intranet failure

The majority of intranet use by event, but the minority by overall duration, is of the targeted information retrieval kind, and therefore carries with it a high expectation of success. This kind of use is on the whole successful and can therefore become habitual. If nothing changes, users will continue with this kind of usage without reflecting on the search capabilities, the navigation structure or the coverage of the intranet. It is the kind of behaviour that subject-orientated users and process-junkies exhibit, and many intranets are established by encouraging it in their initial development of resources, for example internal telephone directories. When an intranet is used for targeted information retrieval, it is successfully fulfilling user needs.

The minority of intranet use by event, but the majority by overall duration, is speculative, and carries with it very little expectation about the specific content recovered. Users may have a concrete conception about the kind of content that they are looking for, but this will not translate into a high expectation of that content being available to them, and therefore their expectation of success in recovering it will be low. Intranet-shy users may exhibit this kind of usage, perhaps reasoning that something might be available, but without having a broad enough conception of the function of the intranet to enable them to be confident in that speculation. Managers often encourage speculative behaviour, justifying that users who understand the coverage of an intranet by engaging in speculative usage are more likely to understand what is available to them and where to find it when they have more concrete information needs. Users generally show a reluctance to use the intranet speculatively, perhaps because they have better ways of spending their time. However, in as much as expectations are not clearly defined, intranets used in this way fulfil the needs of users.

It is when users set out knowing what they want but not knowing where to find it that the intranet is most likely to frustrate their expectations, and they are most likely to notice and be failed by the navigation structure or the search engine. Only expert users have a comprehensive enough understanding of the coverage and organisation of an intranet to make success in goals-orientated usage likely. In all other user groups, perceptions of poor search engines, confusing navigation configurations and incomplete or irrelevant content are formed in this type of behaviour. Failure in this kind of usage can lead to developed expectations of failure in other types of usage, making those expectations endemic. The intranet may serve a range of information needs effectively, as demonstrated above, but because it fails in speculative usage, it may continue to encourage poor perceptions and expectations of failure.

But why do user expectations and intranet delivery diverge in this type of usage? Why does goals-orientated usage fail?

User expectations of intranets

A priori expectations in information seeking

Whenever we use a resource we have a level of expectation of our likelihood of success in finding the information we need. In order to understand our likelihood of success, and adopt appropriate information-seeking strategies, we need to develop a broad understanding of the nature and coverage of the information resource we are approaching. By doing so, we can begin to make realistic judgements about the most appropriate strategies to adopt, and our level of persistence.

For example, when we use a library within an organisation, we develop a level of awareness about its coverage and likely usefulness for different information demands. These expectations precede any explicit demand made upon the resource but develop as a consequence of experience. That experience may be explicit: how we have been served by this resource previously, or implicit: how we have been served by *similar* resources previously. In other words, where we have no explicit experience of the resource in question, we will rely on our experience of similar resources. For example, when we use a library we may have formed a rough idea of what libraries are and what their purpose is from previous experience of libraries. Over time that will migrate to a concrete idea of the services and purpose of the specific library formed on the basis of explicit experience of those services.

Implicit expectations

Users develop much of their implicit a priori expectation of intranets from their experience of the Web. They will predominantly spend more time using the Web than using an intranet, and are likely to develop strategies for finding information on the Web in advance of experiencing intranets. One of the key attractions of intranets for organisations is this assumed level of familiarity, which obviates training considerations.

Most user groups, with the exception of the intranet-shy, will consider themselves skilled in using the Web; they can find what they are looking for most of the time, using a search engine. This encourages a cycle of reinforcement in behavioural patterns for web usage that operates as follows:

1. The abundance of information on the Web means that there is usually something that fulfils a specific information need.

2. Where a resource that will supply the information has not been previously identified, the search engine therefore becomes a more attractive option for finding specific information on the Web than random browsing.

3. Websites are therefore optimised to maximise their position within search engine results, and search engines are optimised to maximise the position of relevant sites using ranking techniques.

4. These ranking techniques remove from the user much of the need to develop more sophisticated search strategies, because in order to maximise returns from search engines and therefore to prioritise the search engines' relevance ranking, broad-based search strategies are more effective.

5. This in turn means that almost *every* use of a web search engine returns an abundance of information.

6. When the required information is not recovered directly by the search engine, the abundance of hits returned by the search strategy and ranking techniques of the search engine mean that one of the returned pages will usually link to the required information.

7. This reinforces the notion that everything is available on the Web, and that the search engine is the best way of locating it.

There is good evidence to suggest broad-based search strategies are preferred on the Web (e.g. Spink, 2004). This is not because users are unable to formulate or unwilling to learn Boolean and proximity searching, or to adopt alternative terminology, but because on the Web basic search strategies work and require less thought. Furthermore, because they work and require less thought they become the preferred strategy of the user, and because this preferred strategy is usually successful it becomes conditioned behaviour. The source of this success is not just the sophistication of search engines, but also the size of the Web. Without sufficient content, search engine ranking methodologies are ineffective. Because Google, the world's most popular search engine (van Vark, 2004), ranks by citation, the more content retrieved matching any given search term, the more effective the ranking technique (Brooks, 2004).

In comparison with the Web, even very large intranets are tiny. However, having honed their skills on the Web, and having developed expectations about successful strategies for HTML-based resources from the Web, users bring with them to intranets their broad-based search strategies. The limited size of intranets means that such strategies fail. Users can be tripped up by basic factors such as their search terms not coinciding with the vocabulary used on a given page. Furthermore, because intranets are small, and because as we shall come to see links between pages on an intranet are necessarily underdeveloped (see Chapter 3), each page has fewer citations, and fewer pages leading to it, which means less chance for the user to find it via an indirect route as a consequence of their basic search strategy.

On well-organised intranets, browsing is a more effective strategy for finding information than searching using a broad-based search strategy. Intranets are generally small enough for their content to be organised in a logical structure that is easy to navigate, but too small for search engines to develop a comprehensive enough index to make relevance ranking techniques truly effective. Yet users consistently prefer searching. Taking away the search engine will not change that preference.

It is not the fault of users that our intranets are an exception to their general rule for finding information on HTML-based resources, and it is not their fault that our intranets do not function as they expect. Intranets look to users like just another Web resource, albeit one that *should* be tailored to their specific needs, on which it *should* be easier to locate information. If it does not work like the Web, they are not inclined to spend much time finding out exactly how it *does* work; they have better things to do. They will stick to their targeted information retrieval behaviour, and when they cannot find information with goals-orientated searching and browsing, they will begin to develop expectations of failure.

Addressing implicit expectations

As information professionals, we are used to searching information systems and getting no results. We use a variety of databases, and are likely to form complex searches to minimise the number of documents recalled and to maximise precision. If we fail, we will try again with a different search strategy. Our experience of information retrieval systems tells us that the failure of a search strategy does not necessarily imply an absence of information. But most intranet users' experience of searching is gained from Web search engines, using broad search strategies designed to maximise recall and minimise precision. Using this approach, it is extremely unlikely that no hits will be found. It is not always the best information that is recovered, it is not always exactly what is needed, but it is rare that an Internet search engine returns nothing. Because of this, intranet users often interpret 'no hits' as 'no information'.

A key goal of search-engine implementation on an intranet is therefore to maximise pages retrieved and to point users to alternative solutions. One way of maximising pages retrieved is to search the Web in parallel with the intranet. Results should be presented side by side on the page, but clearly distinguished. This should end the frustration of searches ending in no hits, and encourage users to use the intranet search for all their needs.

Content creators often have limited web design skills, but it is important that an intranet is managed in such a way as to optimise pages for search engine results. This may be achieved by forcing content creators to add meaningful titles and metadata to pages, and reinforced by regularly auditing pages. Titles should not only be descriptive of the content of a page but also indicative of its location within the broad structure of the intranet. This extra information will aid the user in identifying whether the page is useful to them or not.

To maximise the keywords and synonyms associated with pages, metadata must be added to in a consistent way. If the resources and the technology of the intranet allow, a comprehensive taxonomy covering the organisation's key business interests will help keep this under control, but this should only be considered if you are confident that you will be able to maintain it. An out-of-date or partial taxonomy is worse than no taxonomy, as it will actively mislead the search engine and make searching less efficient.

The value brought by content creators must be measured in terms of usage rather than volume of content created. Contributors to intranets are often satisfied by making information available, and less concerned with maximising usage. They are encouraged in this by the management processes of many intranets (see Chapter 3). Evaluating the performance of content creators in terms of usage and not just content created will help encourage authors to maximise the usability of their information by incorporating meaningful titles and metadata to aid search engine efficiency. Usage should take account of changing and varying levels of demand for different types of information; it should not be derived from a simple hit count.

It should be ensured that individual content providers are given real information about the usage of their site. These usage reports must be presented in a way that is meaningful to content creators. Logs of searches should be kept and analysed. This analysis can be fed directly into the selection of metadata and the maintenance of taxonomies. If searches are consistently constructed with terms that are outside the existing taxonomy, then those terms can be incorporated. This information can also be used to identify changes in the information environment, which may impact directly on the intranet: the users are the real experts on what information they need, and if there is a change in their needs, introduced by either new regulation or legislation, a new area of interest to the organisation or some other factor, this may well show up in the search logs before it reaches the intranet manager by more traditional routes.

Content creators should be discouraged from working in isolation on their own domains of information and encouraged to incorporate as many hyperlinks as possible into their pages. Pages should be created as if they are part of a larger hypertext document called 'the intranet' rather than isolated pieces of information in themselves. Allow users to add comments and links to ordinary intranet pages. This approaches Tim Berners-Lee's original conception of the Web discussed in the introduction. Users are the real experts in the information they utilise; allow them to collaborate with content creators.

Lastly, the search engine must be optimised to take advantage of all these initiatives. Take time to understand how it weights results and test your fine-tuning. On intranets, always give *more* weighting to metadata than you would normally, especially if you have a very tight control over metadata from your use of a content management system or a rigorously imposed taxonomy.

Explicit expectations

Implicit expectations of intranets formed in the use of the Web solidify into explicit expectations as users encounter intranets.

Most users' experience in using the intranet will be in concentrated bursts of targeted information retrieval. When they browse speculatively, it is likely to be within subject areas with which they are familiar. Users may become familiar with those parts of the intranet that are most relevant to their needs, and may even use those parts daily, but still experience the rest of the intranet as an unfamiliar wasteland of information. It is unrealistic to expect all users to become expert users; most, like subject-orientated users and process-junkies, will only ever master what they use frequently. This sedimentation of explicit expectations in daily usage can lead to users seeing pages and navigation structures, but failing fully to comprehend them.

When Tim Berners-Lee coined the phrase 'semantic web' to describe the Web (Berners-Lee, 1999), unconsciously or otherwise he echoed Foucault. However, Foucault meant something different than a web of information linked by semantic associations; he was describing the web of semantic structures by which we organise our understanding of the world: the assumed cognitive paradigms that limit our understanding (Foucault, 2002b). In one sense, hyperlinks create for intranets a framework that defines what it is possible to know about them.

Gestalt theory suggests that we understand the perceivable world through patterning and clustering individual elements of that world. Concepts that are closely associated, whether buttons on a screen or ideas, form a gestalt. The consequence is that human perception is experienced as an interactive process. We bring as much to our perception of the world as we take from visual stimuli. Our perception of the world, and of intranets, is partly formed on the basis of what we expect to see. Once these patterns have formed, they endure beyond the removal of the individual elements that constitute the gestalt. The patterns of previous perception, the expectations of what *should* be experienced, are imposed on what we actually experience.

For intranets this means that as behaviour becomes habitual, users stop noticing the steps they take, stop noticing the components that make up the navigation structures or the pages, and see only what they expect to see until that expectation is overthrown by such a severe change to the intranet that their existing patterns of perception and behaviour no longer function. They will follow the same paths through the intranet every time they use it. They may stick to indirect paths with which they are familiar, even when more direct routes to the information are clearly signposted. Once users have formed their expectations, usually in quite limited parts of the intranet, those expectations will stick. If they find a page has moved, they will be stumped. They will not notice organic changes to the navigation structure of content.

This hard wiring of expectations can lead to false superstitions: behaviour that is linked to outcomes for the user, but which does not influence outcomes. For example, a user who fails to find information on a given subject may develop an understanding that the content does not exist, and continue to believe this even after it has been added. A user who frequently fails to find information by browsing may develop an understanding that the navigation structure does not work. These will harden into expectations of failure. Because of this, all usage becomes orientated about the subject areas and processes that a user understands, and all usage outside those well-understood areas will carry expectations of failure *regardless* of the quality or logic behind the navigation structure or search engine, or the comprehensiveness of the content.

Just because users identify poor content, inadequate search facilities and a lack of structure as the cause of their frustration does not mean that the intranet actually consists of poorly organised content with no adequate search engine. Addressing these elements will therefore only take us so far in solving the problem of low levels of user satisfaction. Users will only ever form concrete expectations of success in those areas of an intranet they understand well and use regularly. Because for the vast majority of users those areas and processes they use regularly make up only a small part of the overall intranet, the intranet as a whole will continue to be perceived by them as confusing and poorly organised.

Addressing explicit user expectations

Do not expect users to change their ways. They will not take time to learn the entire outline of the intranet. Even if you encourage them to do so, that knowledge will quickly become outdated and redundant as the intranet changes, and worse, it will add to their frustrations as their out-of-date knowledge misleads them. Unless they spend a good deal of time browsing the intranet, unless they essentially *become* expert users, they will never get to know anything other than a small part of the intranet sufficiently well to have confidence in it, or to develop realistic expectations about when they can expect to find information successfully. This is not a bad thing. Encourage targeted information retrieval and you will encourage expectations of success.

Make your intranet look small. Even if it has a million pages of information, make it appear to each user as if it has twenty, and not *just* twenty pages, but exactly those twenty pages they need. Users should be under the impression that the intranet is uniquely tailored to their needs. The smaller an intranet appears, the more usable it will be. The more of it that is below the surface, the easier it will be to extract information from it. This may mean personalised content, but many problems can be obviated by good information architecture.

The intranet that is presented to the user should only contain current information that directly supports the jobs of employees and is needed on a day-to-day basis. There is a place on intranets for archival material, there is a place for material that is needed only occasionally and there is a place for material that indirectly supports the jobs of employees, but that place should be out of sight until such time as it is needed. Users should not be presented with links to this less-critical information unless they are looking for it. In practical terms this means relegating a large proportion of the content to a deeper level within the structure.

An intranet that appears small, that promotes up front its business-critical information, will better serve the user. Users will find it easier to locate everyday information and will be prepared to look harder for more unusual information. Put the information that is used every day right at the front, in the face of the user. Do not require users to click more than once to get to it.

Make sure that if users are used to information being in one place, it is always in that place. Do not move it, rename it or change the path to it in any way. It is in using this critical information that the users have most expectation of success. Users will tend to organise their own information environment by bookmarking pages, creating their own resources lists or by remembering URLs. Changing something as simple as a URL may scupper their attempts to use the resource, and because their expectations in this kind of behaviour are so much higher, they will consequently be so much more deterred from further use.

Organise the navigation around user expectations, not around your organisation's internal management structure. Users will not spend much time looking for information they expect to find easily – the heavily in demand information that underpins the function of intranets – so make sure it is near the top of the navigation structure. Conversely, they will be prepared to look harder for information they do not expect to find so readily – the kind of information they may need only occasionally – and this can be placed further down, a few more clicks away. If they have very little or no expectation of finding the information they need on the intranet, they will not look for it. Consequently, design for a small intranet. Do not waste resources creating a vast collection of information that is rarely needed and less used.

Similarly, users are unlikely to know the precise name of a form, for example, nor know or care who is responsible for creating or collating it. Do not make an understanding of organisational structure necessary for locating information by organising your intranet around administrative departments. Your intranet should reflect your users' needs, not the organisation's administrative quirks. Group resources by their function and form. Forms, for example, should be grouped together in your navigation, as should white papers, proposals, procedures manuals, etc., regardless of which department is responsible for collating or maintaining the information. An intranet is an endlessly flexible place; the logical structure does not have to reflect the structure of responsibilities of an organisation. For example, you may organise content creation around departmental sites for administrative convenience, but your navigation should point to information grouped by function rather than sites. For more on this, see Chapter 4.

Summary

Users bring to intranets a series of expectations and patterns of behaviour that need to be accommodated. The use of any information resource is learnt through experience that generates models of expectations. The predominant influence on intranet use is learnt a priori from use of the Web. When users come to intranets, furthermore, they do not usually experience the whole resource, but sections of it. Intranets need to be designed with these factors in mind, limiting the scope of the resource as it is presented to each individual user.

2

Why organisations behave irrationally

Aims

This chapter explores how the intrinsic qualities of organisations generate a complex relationship between information creation, dissemination and use, and how this impacts on the implementation of an intranet. The chapter addresses four areas:

- organisational expectations
- the four functions of intranets
- diverging expectations
- the information wasteland.

Organisational expectations

In the previous chapter we saw how users' expectations of intranets influence their use of those intranets. This chapter looks at intranets from another perspective: what organisations expect their intranets to achieve, and how this influences the implementation of intranets. Organisations, be they commercial, governmental or charitable, anticipate a return on the investment involved in implementing intranets.

That return may be expressed either in financial terms or in intangible benefits. In other words, organisations expect that intranets will either save money, enhance efficiency or both.

For example, an intranet may be planned to reduce the costs of distributing information by reducing printing. An intranet may also be planned to eliminate information black spots, helping ensure that all employees have access to identical information and are making decisions from the same knowledge base. Organisations may justify their intranets as knowledge-sharing tools, perhaps as a part of a wider knowledge management strategy. The intranet may have a role in building organisational identity: in establishing the workplace as a community of shared interest through the media of shared resources.

These organisational expectations translate into four possible functions that intranets can perform.

1. Disseminating information

2. Centrally storing information

3. Facilitating communication

4. Facilitating team-working and knowledge-sharing.

Within individual organisations, objectives may be formulated formally in policy or strategy, or informally, and may include only one or two of the above. However, these points represent the varying expectations that organisations make of intranets.

Are they realistic? Is it realistic to expect, for example, that using an intranet to disseminate information will save money and/or increase efficiency? It is not sufficient to make a connection between the two; that expectation needs to be rationalised. As we dissect these expectations, we will begin to see how the failure of intranets becomes almost inevitable.

The four functions of intranets

Function 1: Disseminating information

Costs associated with the dissemination of information are usually those related to its production and distribution. The intranet will compete with paper-based means of disseminating information because it shares with paper-based information a degree of permanence in that it continues to exist for potential future exploitation beyond the point of its distribution. This can be contrasted, for example, with e-mails, which rely on the archiving practices of individuals for their continued exploitation. For business-critical information such as policies and procedures manuals, the semi-permanence of intranet content makes intranets attractive distribution technologies.

Information is generally cheap to disseminate but expensive to create, regardless of the form in which it is distributed. The costs associated with distributing a paper-based library procedures manual across an organisation, for example, are a fraction of those associated with creating the manual. However, because the costs of producing information are often fixed, relating to the employment of skilled staff, whereas the costs of distributing it are variable or one-off, the tendency of organisations is to focus on the latter rather than the former. It is easier to reduce variable costs than fixed costs.

By comparison, there are minimal variable costs associated with disseminating information electronically. The production costs remain little different from those for paper resources. There is an additional fixed cost in providing the network architecture to allow the information transmission, but this divided between many individual pieces of information adds little to the cost of each, and the network is likely to be already in place and budgeted for. Distributing information electronically can therefore give the appearance of an overall cost reduction, although the extent of this reduction is concealed by the shift in costs from traditional to electronic networks.

As well as decreasing costs, intranets can also be planned to increase efficiency in the exploitation of information. Control over traditionally distributed information is ceded to individuals once it has been disseminated. When it is in their hands, it is largely down to the user to manage that information: to throw out old policy documents, update old procedures manuals and replace old forms. Specific responsibilities for managing important resources may be delegated. However, once information has been distributed, it tends to stay in circulation for longer than may be intended. Invariably, the consequence of giving responsibility to individuals to manage their own information resources is that many versions of the same information coexist. Versions of procedures manuals updated to different points of time can continue in use. Different versions of policy documents can remain in desk drawers or filing cabinets. Updated information can be overlooked or forgotten before it is put into effect.

This is a problem to which an intranet can seem like an ideal solution. An intranet will ensure that everyone has access to the most up-to-date version of a document, and *only* the most up-to-date version. And if people were easily satisfied by this degree of centralised control over their information needs there would be no further problems. Real users, however, tend to organise themselves to their own ends.

These two key advantages of intranets over traditional means of distributing information can fade simply because people do not like searching for the same information time and again, or reading it from screens. As we saw in

Chapter 1, some people are more comfortable in their use of intranets than others, and inevitably those least practised and least skilled – the invisible or shy users – will resort to printing material for future use. However, individual difference is not the only mechanism at work. Computers are interactive tools; people engage with their computers: they adopt a posture that aids that interaction, leaning forward and alert. This posture works against the passive reception of information around which most intranets are designed. When we use computers we are looking to interact, to engage with the screen. When we read passively our posture relaxes, and we sit back. Computers are not designed to carry passively received information, and offices and desks are not designed to encourage this kind of use. As a consequence, users show a reluctance to read from the screen. As users start printing the information on intranets two things are lost:

- the predominant cost advantage of distributing information in electronic rather than paper form;
- control over the version of the information in use.

This causes a further shift from explicit centralised costs to hidden, decentralised costs, which may represent as an overall cost *increase*. One hundred employees individually accessing an intranet, locating a policy document, printing it, wandering over to the printer to collect it, stapling it and filing it is a more expensive means of distributing that information than centralising the process through a print room. The associated staff costs shift from an administrative to a managerial function. The time spent on disseminating information shifts from administrators to the end-users of that information. A saving may appear on the balance sheet, but it is a spectral saving, disappearing in the light.

Function 2: Centrally storing information

Intranets may be intended to act as central stores of information, gathering together in one place the collective knowledge of the organisation. Central information stores implemented in this way become available to users via their desktops. By concentrating all information resources in a single place, users no longer have to decide where to begin searching for information – they need only search the intranet. The function of an intranet of this kind is essentially informative. The reduction of costs involved may arise from the replacement of existing information resources and from the increase in efficiency created by the greater exploitation of existing intellectual and knowledge capital.

Storing information for future use in a single resource is a natural function of an intranet. The origins of HTML lie in Tim Berners-Lee's attempt to organise the information landscape of CERN, making existing information resources more widely accessible, and formulating a universal means of locating resources. The URL, or uniform resource locator, was initially proposed as a *universal* resource locator: a means of referencing information resources regardless of their format or location. The intranet, then, can function to bring together existing information housed in a variety of file formats across a number of information systems.

However, intranets do not merely consist of lists of resources uniformly referenced with a URL. They are webs built on semantic and associative connections. Hyperlinks work best between HTML files; although web browsers will display files in a variety of formats, the file size of many proprietary formats in comparison with HTML means that browsing webs created from Adobe Acrobat or Word documents can be cumbersome. This creates a tension in intranet design between usability through the browsing of HTML pages and the comprehensiveness of access to documentation in other file formats.

One solution is to convert into HTML existing documentation in other file formats. However, there is an intrinsic problem with this. HTML was designed as a general mark-up language allowing information to be accessed across platforms. In other words, HTML is not very powerful in its presentational flexibility. Therefore much corporate documentation will necessarily need to be stored and used in proprietary formats such as Word or Excel, and will consequently be prepared in those formats. Converting them subsequently to HTML introduces a new cost into the dissemination of that information. There are further questions as to whether converting files adequately exploits the potential of HTML, whether HTML is adequately able to present information designed for other media and formats, and therefore whether there is not also an efficiency cost in presenting information designed for other formats as HTML.

A second solution is to produce all documentation in HTML in the first place. Although this may be adequate for internal documentation such as forms or policy statements, it is likely that there will remain much material for which HTML is not suitable because of its limited presentation capabilities, for example material intended for external consumption.

A third solution is to house both an HTML version of each document alongside the original in proprietary format. For example, an HTML version of a report may be housed on the intranet for quick reference and hyperlinks incorporated into it where appropriate enabling it to function as true hypertext, but a link to the original version may also be supplied for circumstances in which control over the presentation of the material is important. However, the non-linear structure of hypertext documents is different from the linear structure of traditional paper-based documents, and there will necessarily be a compromise in this approach between enabling documents to function as true hypertext and enabling them to function as paper-based resources.

What is clear is that making an intranet work as a central store of information requires considerable investment in the preparation of that information for the intranet environment. This introduces costs that may not be foreseen, and changes the relationship between the cost and efficiency savings generated by making this corporate knowledge more widely available. These extra costs can be overcome entirely by supplying new documents in their original format; however, the whole point of HTML, the whole point of hypertext, and by extension the justification for intranets, are the semantic and associative connections between information that we term hyperlinks. Without those connections, an electronic collection of documents is not necessarily any more useful or any more likely to encourage the exploitation of existing knowledge capital than paper documents in filing cabinets.

Function 3: Facilitating communication

Intranets are ineffective communications tools. Some communication media and their qualities are summarised in Table 2.1. For example, telephones strip us of visual clues to the content or meaning of the message being communicated, but they are a two-way medium in real time enabling instant feedback and allowing the communicator to judge the reception of the message being communicated. Telephones are time-intensive and can only be conducted on a one-to-one or one-to-few (with conference calling) basis. However, for some purposes this depersonalisation is desirable.

By contrast, intranets are poor communication tools. There are no adequate feedback mechanisms allowing

| Table 2.1 | Communications channels |

	One to one?	One to many?	Real-time feedback?	Delayed feedback?	Initiated by?	Guaranteed reception?
Face to face	Yes	Yes	Yes	Yes	Speaker	Yes
Telephone	Yes	One to several	Yes	Yes	Speaker	Yes
E-mail	Yes	Yes	No	Yes	Sender	Yes
Printed memo	Yes	Yes	No	Limited	Sender	No
Intranet	No	Yes	No	Limited	Reader	No

messages to be modulated as they are communicated. Such feedback mechanisms that do exist, such as e-mail links and web-forms, are wholly inadequate for gaining true information about how the message has been received, because they introduce an extra barrier to that feedback. (Unlike e-mail the act of replying is not well integrated into the form of the original message.) There is no way of guaranteeing that your message will get through.

Just because the intranet is on everyone's desktop and includes bulleted 'what's new' information directing users to the communication does not mean that messages communicated on an intranet have a good chance of reaching a large audience. As we have seen with user behaviour, the intranet can become like wallpaper. People become so used to the home page that they no longer see what is there – they see only what they expect to be there. They stop reading the text and start relying on their familiarity with the layout and navigation to find what they want. Use an active desktop to deliver information and over time the same tendency will reassert itself. It should be assumed that nothing on an intranet will be read without the user actively looking for it.

These weaknesses of intranets as communication tools can be overcome by introducing novelty. For example, an animation will work to draw users' attention to changing information. However, using the same animation over a period of time will lessen its effectiveness. You can change the entire design of the home page and force the users to reassess its content, but this will irritate them because they are being required to work at a fresh understanding of the resource. One of the most efficient ways of communicating business-critical messages is temporarily to hijack the active desktop or intranet home page, but in doing so the intranet is essentially being turned into a communications channel. If you take over the home page of your intranet for your vital communications too often, not only will it lose impact as a means of communicating vital information, it will also impair the usability of the intranet as an information tool.

This is not to say that intranets have no role as communications devices, but it must be recognised that in order for any individual to receive a communication via an intranet, they have actively to look for it, which means they have to have an identifiable need or be a part of a community of interest. The kinds of information that intranets are excellent for communicating include:

- Non-critical information that still needs to be communicated, for example new contract wins. The advantage of using an intranet to communicate this kind of information is that it fulfils the organisation's objective of keeping staff informed without actually impacting upon the staff in an intrusive way.

- Information for which there is a community of interest within the organisation – information that is important to groups within the organisation, but not necessarily to the whole organisation.

- Information communicated *between* individuals and groups within an organisation, particularly with the use of document and file sharing, or discussion groups.

Generally speaking, however, the expectation that an intranet will save money by replacing existing communications channels and increase efficiency by streamlining communication through one medium is founded on a misconception. It is predicated on the assumption that there is no fundamental difference in the effectiveness of different types of communications media for different purposes.

Function 4: Facilitating team-working and knowledge-sharing

The tendency for individual employees to create their own archives of material has motivated the development of knowledge management, and by extension intranets. The corporate memory can become fragmented across individually managed pools of knowledge. Although these individual pools of knowledge may continue to feed into the productivity of the organisation through the conduit of the individuals and departments that have collated them, the informal processes by which this happens leads to fragmented information provision and patchy exploitation of the intellectual resources of the organisation.

The intranet has a vital role in the implementation of knowledge management practices. However, it is not a replacement for knowledge management practices, nor is it on its own a knowledge management tool. The intranet will only facilitate team-working and knowledge-sharing as a part of a wider knowledge management approach.

Teams and knowledge are qualities of people. People are unpredictable in the way in which they relate to each other, and their behaviour can be irrational or self-defeating. However, they primarily relate to each other through face-to-face contact, and secondarily through modes of communication that capture some of the qualities of that face-to-face contact, such as the telephone or e-mail. Intranets are more effective as information not communication tools, as we have seen. The way in which the individuals within an organisation relate to each other, and the preconceptions or expectations they bring with them regarding the function or purpose of that communication within the organisation, is a question of culture, and culture is developed over a long time and learned through collective experience.

An intranet will mirror the prevailing culture of the organisation, not define it. People will not choose their modes of communication on the basis of what they experience on the intranet, but rather on the basis of what they experience in their surroundings. If there is a managerial impetus to shift the prevailing modes of communication from a closed competitive culture to an open sharing culture, an intranet can be used as a part of this process, but the overwhelming change that is required is cultural not informational. An intranet will not bring about an instant exploitation of existing intellectual and knowledge capital within the organisation, and therefore without an investment in cultural change little efficiency gain from the exploitation of that capital can be expected from intranets.

Diverging expectations

Three things should be apparent from the above:

- Organisational expectations can be unrealistic if couched in broad terms. An intranet cannot be expected to improve communications, for example, without consideration of the means by which it can do this in the light of other communications channels.

- Organisational expectations broadly defined conflict with the behaviour of users. Users' expectations are practical, organisations' expections strategic. There is an inherent tension between these different formulations of individual- and organisation-orientated expectation.

- The expectations of organisations are a combination of various functions *within* the organisation, such as information provision or internal promotion, which are likely to be the responsibility of, or at least performed by, different departments or individuals within that organisation. For example, communal identity and social cohesion are likely to be the responsibility of groups within an organisation different to those for the dissemination of information or maintenance of an information collection. No single part of the organisation will share in all the expectation or demands made of the intranet, and very often these different demands will conflict.

Organisations are not cohesive bodies with unified needs or interests. An organisation begins with the individuals who make up that organisation. Each of those individuals has their own motivations for working within the framework of the organisation: their own intrinsic self-interest.

Those individuals usually form into groups within departments, service lines, support lines or other groupings. These groups may be expressed formally through the departmental structure of an organisation or they may be expressed informally through alignments of common interests. Usually there will be a mixture of formal and informal groups within any organisation, and any individual may be a member of a number of groups with overlapping interests. For example, a subject librarian is a member of a subject team, a community of interest around that subject, the library team and various other groups within a university, and each of these implies different allegiances and communities of interest. Each of these groupings within any organisation will have its own perspective, self-interest and corner to fight. Organisations can be viewed as overlapping communities of interest, and this creates a tension in the management of intranets.

These competing expectations affect intranets differently than other information resources, such as libraries, because people *go* to a library but an intranet comes to them. When using a library, or a research service, there is a tacit acceptance of the terms of the service as it is provided. The service is always *owned* by someone else, and the individual buys into that service with a hope of achieving their ends, creating a temporary alliance of interest. Intranets are different. Those formal or informal groupings within an organisation are in part responsible for the intranet content they use and publish. Intranets are owned by everyone.

The information wasteland

The four expectations discussed in this chapter can create a conflict in the implementation of intranets from the tension between the qualities of information determined by these objectives. This effect can be clearly seen in the tension between the intranet as a central storehouse of information and as a way of disseminating information. Information currency is central to this tension. Old reports, old letters or old data are often indicative of work done, of past success, of the significant contribution of a group within an organisation to the organisation's success. And because there is very often no other place for old information, it can end up on the intranet.

There is a value in this record of things done, a value in a corporate memory of not only what has been achieved in the past but also the way in which it was achieved. This corporate memory can point the way to new successes and to improving current practice. It can identify the experts in any given field within the organisation: those who have the experience or expertise to tackle current issues. It can map out existing practices: the way in which things are done and the way they should continue to be done. It can record in shared experience those problems that crop up only occasionally, so that the solutions need not be reinvented every few years. There is indeed a value in this old information. Or at least, there is a value in some of it, and it is difficult to predict which of it will become valuable in the future.

For the most part, however, this corporate memory serves little function. It is largely archived away – be that formally on CD-ROMs in India, for example, well classified and stored, or informally in the desk drawers of employees. Most of it will play no further part outside of the context for which it was originally produced. The reason that traditionally this archived corporate memory is able to lie dormant until it is really needed is precisely because of the method of its storage. Old files in basements, or on CD-ROMs in Luton or in India, for example, do not impinge on the day-to-day function of the organisation (although they may of course cause their own problems).

Imagine that this corporate memory was not stored in these formal or informal archives, but that every file that crossed an employee's desk stayed on their desk. Imagine that the only archive of the organisation's past practice was the in-tray – that every report or white paper stayed in some way current until disposed of entirely, stayed a part of day-to-day business processes until deleted from stock. Although making the intellectual property of the organisation available, faced with this situation individual employees would soon sink beneath a mire of information, hampered at every turn in selecting what they need now, this second, from what they may need in an hour, a week, a month, a year's time or never at all.

No organisation works like this, but many intranets do. It is not a failure to distinguish 'what's new' from what is not that creates the problems, it is the shared space for current, everyday information – the stuff I need now to do my job now – and the corporate memory – the stuff I needed once and may perhaps need at some undetermined point in the future. It is the tension between the expectation that an intranet will disseminate current information and act as a central store for all other information. This tension leads to a lack of clarity of purpose. Old information that would once have made up the corporate memory is kept side by side with current information in active circulation. Without clearly signposting the different qualities of information, many intranets become information wastelands, where the corporate memory smothers current concerns.

Similarly, the communicative function can become confused with the informative function. The intranet becomes an easy solution to the dissemination of information. Putting something on the intranet can too often be seen as the end of the process rather than the beginning. Individuals who have some responsibility for making some information available to the rest of the organisation, or some responsibility for *communicating* some particular issue, can too easily fall back on publishing that information on an intranet and regarding the job as done.

Is lodging something on an intranet actually *communicating*? In that there are those within an organisation who will make it their responsibility to keep up to date, it is. But there is here a fundamental shift in responsibility from the communicator of information to the receiver: it is no longer the responsibility of the person who owns the information to communicate its existence; it becomes the responsibility of the individual to become informed. The informative process has replaced the communicative process, and in many organisations this is enacted under the guise of a *communications* policy, a *communications* function. Some employees will view it as a part of their role to stay informed, some will not. Some will feel comfortable with an intranet as a mechanism for staying informed, some will not. The ends of individual responsibility are not the issue here, rather the tendency for organisations essentially to wash their hands of the responsibility for communicating effectively with employees. Making information available is not the same as communicating it.

Intranets can therefore become information wastelands, where content is published as a cheaper alternative to properly informing employees. They can become information wastelands where employees view publishing content as the end of their responsibility – direct quantifiable evidence that they have performed their role of making information available without any real care as to whether that information is useful in the form in which it has been published. Intranets can become a mechanistic way of demonstrating and recording achievement.

This process occurs because organisations expect their intranets to do too much. They expect them to fulfil the four functions outlined above, without exploring not only how well the intranet can achieve each in comparison with other information and communications tools, but also to what extent the expectations informing those functions conflict. The single platform for all information needs becomes a confusing aggregate of different types of information with different functions and different characteristics, all presented to the user as if they are of the same value. It is no wonder that users find intranets confusing and difficult to use.

Solutions

Solutions can be implemented to tackle the issues raised above. Some are practical and relate to actual intranet implementation. Some are structural and relate to organisational and managerial expectations of intranets.

Structural solutions

A communications policy should be created or adapted to incorporate the intranet. Different types of information must be distinguished and the best means of communicating each formally decided. Some information may suit traditional methods, such as meetings, memos and newsletters; other information may suit electronic methods such as e-mail, desktop bulletins or the intranet itself. Communication channels can be integrated with the intranet by, for example, using e-mail to *communicate* an important piece of information and the intranet to *inform* users further by allowing access to more information through an embedded link.

Ensure the intranet *is* current and *does* inform. This not only covers set procedures for determining the archiving of old material, it means overcoming the temptation to resort to the mantra 'it's on the intranet', overcoming the temptation to view publishing information on the intranet as the end of the job rather than the beginning.

Confront the shift in tangible costs to hidden costs brought about by intranets. Not tackling this issue will make eventual perceptions of failure inevitable, because in the pursuit of a reduction in tangible costs the intranet will in effect make the day-to-day jobs of most employees more difficult.

Allow usage to become elective by encouraging the informative role of the intranet over the communicative. Do not try to force user behaviour by removing all other formats of the information (such as paper-based manuals). Users will rebel by printing out the intranet version for future use. Do not offer incentives to use the intranet, such as competitions or prizes, because users will use the intranets while those incentives are in place, but return to their old, effective habits once they have been removed, and in this process they may gain an understanding of the intranet that is fixed in time and that impedes their future use. Users need to be encouraged to *elect* to use an intranet resource by making it intrinsically useful to them at the time that they need information, or less effort than alternative solutions.

Practical solutions

Reconfigure the information on the intranet to take advantage of what intranets do well. Information on an intranet must be presented in a way that allows employees actively to engage with it rather than passively to receive it. If there is a reason for people to prefer the electronic form, a real advantage to keeping it in electronic form rather than printing it, they will use it in that form. Employees will act to maximise their own efficiency: if it is more efficient for them to use the information as it appears on the intranet and to go back to the intranet to use it time and time again, they will do exactly that.

When you build intranet-based information resources it is essential that they work *as* hypertext rather than reproducing existing paper documentation in electronic form. Intranet content must fully exploit intranet technology and be built around the tasks that computers are good at performing rather than the processes in which paper-based resources succeed. It is not enough to upload paper-based documentation onto an intranet. Most existing corporate documentation was developed within a paper culture and is designed to work as a paper-based resource. It may be wordy with a strongly linear structure, require little decision-making and offer little scope for interaction. Give users a reason to prefer the electronic resource – they will not automatically prefer it because it is electronic. There is already a reluctance to engage with information in electronic form. Take advantage of that reluctance by seizing the opportunity to recast the corporate information resource in a more usable form. That means that corporate documentation must be written for the Web. The intranet must become its primary form, and that must be reflected in the processes by which the documentation is brought into being.

There are principles to writing for web resources; these are outlined in many good design manuals, some of which are given in the resource list at the end of this book. There is not room enough to go into them here in any depth. However, some important points can be made:

- Break information down into smaller chunks, and use the hyperlinks to build semantic relationships between these chunks that go beyond the linear structure of paper-based documentation.

- Ensure that each document works as hypertext by ensuring that content creators link to other information both *within* the document and *outside* of it. Documents should be written as hypertext, not converted to hypertext from other formats. This will encourage non-linear structures.

- Make a print-optimised version available. This may be achieved by allowing users to interact with the text using a tick-box menu to select those components of a larger document they require in their printed version. This will enable them to exploit the information as an electronic resource rather than an electronic copy of a paper resource. If users can compile and recompile the information to suit their specific needs under different circumstances, they will return to the electronic text habitually because the control they have over that information will be intrinsically valuable in electronic form.

- Keep Adobe Acrobat documents, word processor documents, spreadsheets and formats other than HTML away from the surface level of your intranet unless you can justify in each case exactly why the information needs to be in this format. Even where there is a real or compelling need to have information in alternative formats, incorporate this as a file linked from an HTML version of the same information. There are very few *good* reasons for including alternative document formats on your intranet. If there is a compelling reason why information must be presented in a certain form, then an intranet may not be the best way of distributing it.

- Allow users to fill in and post forms online. For forms that go through an approval process, build that approval process into an electronic form so that it is automatically sent for approval when an employee clicks on Submit. It is not intrinsically more efficient for users to download and print forms than have them available in a stationary cupboard. Making forms available for downloading is only going half way to true implementation of an electronic information resource.

These are just a few examples covering some of the most common information resources available on an intranet. The common thread that must run through all intranet content is this: exploit the power of electronic resources to give control and power to the user in their selection and compilation of the information they use. Do not simply reproduce paper documentation in another form. Do not dump your paper resources on an intranet in the hope that it will save production costs. Exploit the strengths of the technology.

Allow users to become active participants in the information they use by personalising content. People are used to being able to tell computers what to do. They are used to interacting with computers. Let the user take control of this process.

Archival material, if it forms part of an intranet, must be kept separately. It should not appear under the normal navigation structure. It should not crop up in the normal search. Users must be expected to make a conscious effort to look for archival material, not simply come across it when they are looking for that current information they need to do their job now. It may seem that making a structural distinction between archival and current content would reduce exploitation of the corporate memory, but just like shifting old files from your in-tray to a properly organised filing system, the reverse is true – it will make it more effective.

Whenever *you* communicate with employees about the function of the intranet, ensure there is a clear distinction made between the role of the intranet in providing current information as a tool in the business process and the role of the archive in acting as a corporate memory. The roles and functions of the two will become confused if the message is that the archive is available on the intranet.

Summary

The expectations that organisations have of intranets introduce inherent conflicts in their function. Intranets are expected to do several things simultaneously under the umbrella of a single resource: to merge the communicative function and the informative function; to do things cheaper and do things better; to disseminate new information and store old information, etc. These expectations can be couched in vague or unrealistic terms. Organisations often expect intranets to take over existing functions, such as dissemination of information, without affecting the nature of those functions. For example, paper resources are migrated to intranets with little or no modification. A framework describing what intranets do well, in parallel with what other information processes do well, needs to be established in order to set objectives for intranets realistically.

3

Reconciling competing expectations

Aims

Chapters 1 and 2 have examined the ways in which user and organisational expectations can undermine the success of intranet projects. This chapter examines the process of reconciling those competing expectations. So far we have concentrated on two key areas, user and organisational behaviour, and suggested solutions for managing expectations that work within each of these areas. In order to create a truly successful intranet, we need to develop ways of managing intranets that cut across these issues, ways of reconciling competing expectations and of building solutions that knit together the fragmentation of needs represented in the interests of these various groups. The chapter explores five areas:

- organisation structure and information ownership
- defining competing expectations
- the roles people play
- why competing expectations lead to failing intranets
- managing competing expectations.

Organisational structure and information ownership

The old adage 'information is power' is not quite applicable to the modern information age, though it does come close. As the developed world has shifted from industrial production to service industries, the role of information in the economy has become more pronounced. Entire sectors, such as accountancy, financial services, management consultancy, web enterprises, employment consultancy and journalism, are founded on the processing of information, and in many other sectors, such as health-care, industry and retail, information plays a significant part. In the twenty-first century, everybody is an information professional.

The difference between the function of information in these sectors and in formal information work, or in other words the difference between the accountant and the librarian, is that other professions see information as a means to an end, whereas for information professionals the information is the end. For example, auditors do nothing but process information. They source information from their client accounts, and combine that with information from regulatory sources and professional expertise. Within that process they predominantly deal with a narrow range of information from clearly defined sources orientated around their professional role. Much of that information is familiar, well understood and used routinely. For information professionals, however, there is a greater diversity in the types and sources of the information they will manage, and a greater familiarity with those sources, but less familiarity with the actual information itself.

Intranets are built from the ordinary everyday information that oils the processes of business and workplaces. They are not built from the unusual, difficult to find or occasional information that information professionals have traditionally managed. People will not go to intranets for such information; they will go to libraries, to the Web or to their colleagues.

Therefore the intrinsic groupings within an organisation, the alliances of shared interests and the conflicting perspectives on ownership of information processes play a bigger part in managing intranets than in managing traditional information collections. Information may not quite equate to power, but the information and processes used within a department are the keys to unlocking those alliances of shared interest, and by ceding control of those processes, individuals and groups can feel they are losing their role within an organisation. The competition over information ownership that is engendered defines the management of intranets.

Expectations defined

What people expect an intranet to achieve, what they expect it to do for them, depends upon their role within an organisation. There are four principal roles that individuals adopt in relation to intranets:

- strategic management
- intranet management
- content creation
- user.

These may be represented in the management pyramid shown in Figure 3.1. The majority of the people within an organisation will have a direct relationship with the intranet as users. A smaller number of people, but still a significant

Figure 3.1 Roles in relation to intranets

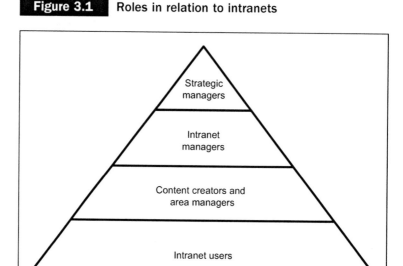

group, will be involved in the content creation process, usually from the perspective of a departmental group. Relatively fewer people will view the intranet from a broader strategic management perspective – not just as a tool for solving specific information needs, but as a means of fulfilling the organisation's objectives.

Each of these groups has a different perspective on the function of the intranet within the organisation. Their perspectives are informed by different objectives. Much of this will depend on the specifics of the organisation itself, and processes such as information audits may help to bring some of this to the surface. However, some general comments can be made.

Strategic management

This first group comprises people who have a strategic or managerial responsibility over some of the functions of the intranet, although no direct responsibility for managing the intranet itself. For example, a director of communications may not have a direct input in the management of an intranet project, but may expect an indirect influence on those aspects of intranet implementation that explicitly or implicitly impinge on the broader communications remit. The people who make up this group have an intrinsic interest because they have overall responsibility for something the intranet does or should be doing. They are likely to consist of those senior managers within an organisation who have some responsibility for the four functions of an intranet we referred to in Chapter 2. These are the people meant when 'management buy-in' is discussed.

Strategic managers are a small but influential group. The expectations that they have may generically be termed *strategic*, in other words they are focused on *outcomes* and not necessarily on the practicalities of achieving those outcomes. For example, a finance director or manager may not care explicitly *how* the intranet achieves a cost saving in the distribution of information, just that it does. Because strategic managers may not have an absolute grasp of the detail of intranet implementation, their expectations about what may be realistically achieved may be framed in either relatively loose or budgetary terms. In other words, the key questions they will want answering are:

- *How much will it cost?*
- *What will it do?*

Intranet managers

Intranet managers will have the most direct influence on the direction and form of the intranet, and will have a very good understanding of the broad coverage and content of the intranet, but may not have an entirely clear understanding of how each part of it is used in the business process. Their skills and experience are unlikely to be allied to the core business of the organisation: for example, intranet managers within financial services firms are unlikely to be financial advisers, and intranet managers within charities are unlikely to be public-sector administrators. Most intranet managers will themselves be expert users, and so they may overlook the difficulties of other user groups. As a consequence of these two factors, their understanding of the role the intranet plays within the business of the organisation may be some-what detached or idealised.

Intranet managers are likely to be a small group, perhaps even a group of one. Their influence on intranet implementation is strong but may be restricted by terms of reference dictated by strategic managers. Where responsibility for aspects of intranet management is divided between several people, each acting as a specialist, intranet management expectations can become fragmented. For example, an information professional will have a different perspective on management priorities for an intranet than an IT professional.

Content creators and managers

Content creators and content-area managers may individu-ally be responsible for only a fraction of the overall content that is available on an intranet; however, collectively they provide the major day-to-day influence on that content. They differ from the management group in that their intrinsic interest is neither global nor strategic, but focused on those parts for which they are responsible. They may not care a great deal about the functionality of other parts of the intra-net, as long as the part with which they are involved works, or at least, as long as they *think* it works. Content creators are often focused on *solutions*, i.e. they have something concrete that they want to achieve and view the intranet as a possible solution. For example, they may be responsible in a broader context for making available employment policies and documents, or for maintaining staff skills records, and regard the intranet as a practical means of fulfilling that responsibility. Those solutions can often be task-orientated, rather than user-orientated. In other words, content creators can focus on achieving tasks rather than on enabling users.

Unlike intranet managers, they may prefer other solutions over the intranet if they judge that they are likely to be more successful or involve less work. They are unlikely to view the solutions they implement in terms of the broader strategic goals of the organisation, but rather in terms of what works best for any given problem they face at that time. They will be reluctant to implement strategies to bene-fit the wider organisation that are unfit for their own needs. For example, departmental content creators who are used to producing a department-wide current awareness briefing via e-mail will not necessarily migrate to an intranet solution unless they see real benefits for their department or them-selves in doing so, despite wider strategic policies.

Content creators and content-area managers are likely to have other demands on their time, and will not view the intranet as their highest priority. Their primary responsibi-lity may be for fulfilling a wider information need, and the intranet may be a means to this end. This contrasts with intranet managers, for whom the intranet is the end of their responsibility.

Intranet users

The fourth group consists of users. Users form the largest of the four groups, and their expectations are *practically orientated*, i.e. they have some information requirement that they need to fulfil and they will do so in the easiest, most convenient way they can at the time that requirement presents itself. Whereas intranet managers and content creators have a common interest in the intranet itself, albeit a differently focused interest, users have no real interest in the intranet for its own sake. Issues relating to user perspectives are discussed in Chapter 1.

The roles people play

The four roles discussed above are summarised in Table 3.1. Individuals may belong to several of these groups at different times or concurrently. For example, a communications director is also a user when wanting to find a phone number; content creators are also users of that content for which they are not responsible. Individuals may bring expectations from their different roles into their other roles, and this may, for example, alter the substance of their usage or their perspective as a manager.

Implicit in the above are four types of expectations that are made of intranets: strategic expectations, for example:

Table 3.1   The roles people play

Group	Size	Expectations
Strategic managers	Small	Strategy orientated
Intranet managers	Small	Intranet orientated
Content creators	Large	Solutions orientated
Users	Largest	Practically orientated

'how does the intranet fit in with a broader communications strategy?'; solutions-orientated expectations, for example: 'how do I send out this communications strategy document?'; intranet-orientated expectations, for example: 'how would publishing this communications strategy document work towards the aims of the intranet?'; and practical expectations, for example: 'where can I get that communications strategy document?'

Ideally, as in the example here, those four sets of expectations align sufficiently that they can all be satisfied in the same process. However, this is not always the case. The content creator can fulfil their strategic need to make information available on one level without concerning themselves with whether that information is accessible or usable to a wider audience. These limited expectations can cascade down the management pyramid. For example, a strategic manager may identify a goal of implementing an intranet site to cover their area of responsibility, perhaps because other departments have sites and there is an organisation-wide push on initiatives to improve communication which has resulted in pressure from various sources for him or her to do something, and an intranet site is something that can be done. That loosely defined strategic aim may be translated into an objective for the content manager to produce a site, which may be translated into an objective for the content creator to collate and publish material relating to a specific content area. Everyone in this process has narrowly defined objectives within a broad strategic remit and been able to achieve their aims successfully. However, the actual *usability* of the information is beyond their terms of reference. The information has been made available not for the benefit of users but for the benefit of managers.

It is in this process of translating strategic objectives into concrete information architecture that the usability of intranets can be lost. They become information wastelands, because making information available becomes enough to fulfil poorly defined objectives. They become fragmented because supplying the information needs of a single community is enough to fulfil poorly defined objectives. They become splintered because content creators working within the framework of what *they* are responsible for, what *they* have to justify as time well spent, are always going to incorporate more semantic or associative structure within that content for which they are responsible than between it and content from other sources. They become battlefields for competition in information ownership, as strategic objectives become translated into concrete solutions *within* the context of identifiable content areas with a specific audience and specific problems for which to find solutions.

Hypertext or bust

One of the inevitable consequences of organising the function of intranets around an existing department or group is that it reinforces the sense of departmental or group ownership of information and information processes. There is both a macro and a micro consequence of this.

- On the macro level, intranets can encourage a kind of information turf-warfare rather than the open and sharing information environment that is often imagined of them. Different interest groups within an organisation may have overlapping information needs, which is where the potential for sharing information resources originates. But these needs are overlapping, not identical. Very often the processes that govern that information – the ways in which it is used and therefore its most important inherent qualities – vary across departments even when the raw information need is analogous. This can create competition over the ownership of information and information processes between interested parties. Traditionally, this competition results in duplication of effort in collating and processing information as each department or interest group attends to its needs. With intranets, the express desire to reduce duplication of effort can result in tension about who precisely is best suited to manage different information resources.

- The micro level consequence occurs at the point at which the user enters the equation. By organising intranets around organisational functions, the user is required to understand how the organisation is structured, with all the irregular and perhaps irrational idiosyncrasies that may have developed over time, before they are able to understand fully how information is arranged on the intranet.

Hypertext was intended to overcome this. The idea behind hypertext is that information is organised by semantic relationships rather than by hierarchical principles. For example, an expenses form may ultimately be the responsibility of the payroll department, and consequently may be accessible on an intranet only via a subsite of the payroll department. However, a semantic connection can be made between expenses and human resources policies, and a hyperlink put in to connect the two pieces of information. As a consequence, users need not necessarily know who is responsible for any given piece of information, or necessarily where it is housed; they can search for that information by making an association with another piece of information.

Hyperlinks can either be vertical, travelling up and down the hierarchical structure of an intranet from top-level sites through departmental sites down to individual pages, or they can be horizontal, cutting across this hierarchical structure. The first kind of hyperlink forms a hierarchical structure – usually modelled on the departmental structure of the organisation. The second kind forms a semantic and associative structure that breaks the mould of the organisation's internal structure to create links between information on the basis of the semantic association of that information – on the basis of what it has in common, not who owns or is responsible for it.

In theory, the more developed this semantic structure of an intranet is, the better it will function. In other words, the more horizontal hyperlinks there are the better. In reality, different groups within an organisation develop their own sense of ownership over information. Just as the organisation relies on the exploitation of its intellectual capital, so too do these individual groups. This means that hyperlinks between distinct content areas can be minimal, or non-existent, causing the hierarchical structure of the intranet to become the only effective navigational aid. The very reason for using hypertext is lost.

There are two main reasons for this. The first is explicable and straightforward, the second more complicated.

1. Content creators are naturally far more likely to understand the scope and arrangement of the content within their own content area. They are naturally less likely to understand the scope and arrangement of the information in other content areas. This is not only because their direct involvement in the creation of a content area reinforces their understanding of that content area over others, but also because the content area for which they are responsible is likely in some way to reflect their broader role or expertise. This has the consequence of reinforcing the allegiance of content creators to their department over

their allegiance to the organisation, or at least of reinforcing the *appearance* of this allegiance.

2. Because content creators are likely to share in the identity of the group for whom they are creating intranet content, there is a tendency for them to protect that group identity and to promote the interests of the group above those of the organisation as a whole. The practical consequence is that even where departments or groups share information by publishing it on intranets, they effectively hoard information by competing for ownership of it, and by promoting the hierarchical structure of that information over the semantic and associative structures. In other words, it can be in the interests of content creators to make hyperlinks only *within* those department information structures rather than across them, because they identify the information as being their possession. Horizontal hyperlinks can threaten that sense of ownership because the information may lose the full context of its setting.

The fallout from this for intranet management is that individual content creators are more likely to hyperlink *within* the confines of the structures they have a close association with and understanding of – their department or grouping – and conversely less likely to hyperlink *outside* of those structures. In other words, the natural tendency for content creators is to reinforce the structures of the organisation within the intranet content they create – to reinforce the hierarchical rather than the semantic or associative structures of information.

These factors result in intranets that are made up of dozens of small sites with few connections interlinking them; an intranet that in its architecture perfectly reflects the organisational structure; an intranet that lacks those semantic and associative links between information; an intranet that reinforces the departmental and individual ownership of intellectual capital; and worst of all, an intranet that advertises the fragmentation of the organisation to anyone who cares to look.

Why competing expectations cause intranets to fail

Intranets may consist predominantly of a number of individual content areas targeted at specific groups within the wider community that are produced *within* that group for the *benefit* of that group, e.g. departmental sites. Groups within the organisation whose remit includes informing the entire organisation will be more successful at creating intranet content areas that are orientated towards single groups. Intranet content areas are successful to greater or lesser degrees in achieving their objectives of supplying information to a targeted group, depending on the competence of the management and production processes involved. These are easy to improve, and largely a matter of competent information architecture and web design, on which an abundance of material is available.

Intranets also consist of efforts to provide coherence across these content areas, which may be more or less successful. These attempts are complicated by the fact that the requirements of addressing a specific audience may be different from those of addressing a wider audience. Users may exploit those parts of an intranet targeted at them with a great deal of competence, and yet still feel that the intranet as a whole is a sea of redundant, confusing information, because those parts that are not addressed directly at them remain intimidating or difficult to understand, as we have seen in Chapter 1. Content areas may contain information structures that are built around the needs of another group, and may use terminology or jargon that acts as convenient shorthand for that other group. They may even be actively hostile to users outside of the group for which they are intended.

There is significant overlap between the type of information a member of one group may need from a content area and the type someone outside that group may need. For example, information about the specific skills of the employees within a group such as a department is likely to be as valuable to the wider members of the organisation as to the department itself. There may also be considerable overlap *between* content areas, for example the needs of one group may partly reflect the needs of another (Figure 3.2). Therefore, intranets that are allowed to develop as collections of content areas managed independently are intrinsically inefficient in their tendency to duplicate materials and effort. Duplication of materials and effort reintroduces the

Figure 3.2　Content shared between areas

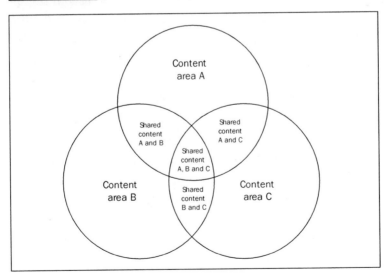

problem created by two versions of the same information existing concurrently but giving an explicitly or implicitly different message. Intranets therefore require managing to introduce a degree of coherence and structure between content areas. This usually involves identifying where information needs are shared between groups, as in Figure 3.2. However, this attempt to introduce coherence and structure can act to fragment information resources for the individual user. By defining exactly who is responsible for what information, for example, users now have to contend with finding information that may previously have been mediated through a single content area targeted at their specific needs.

In theory, the semantic and associative structure of hypertext should allow that fragmentation to be overcome. However, as we have seen, the lack of motivation for content creators and managers to create these semantic and associative links, not to mention their own difficulties in navigating the wider information terrain, mean that in practice this will not occur. Content creators are unlikely to provide those semantic and associative links, and because their remit has been restricted in an effort to create greater intranet-wide coherence and structure by defining exactly what content they may provide, the coverage of these content areas will decrease. Intranets become less useful to users as each content area contains only a part of the information they need. Rather than have their information needs mediated by content areas, users now have to contend with seeking out the information they need across the intranet.

In other words, managing intranets to reduce duplication of materials and effort can make them less effective for the user. Chapters 5 and 6 outline how to tackle and overcome some of these issues while implementing or revamping intranets. The remainder of this chapter focuses on some limited approaches to reconciling these competing expectations.

Managing competing expectations

Defining expectations

The most important part of reconciling these competing expectations is demarcating the roles and responsibilities of those involved with an intranet project. This demarcation should be performed on the basis of the expectations of the different groups outlined above. For example, the influence of strategic management needs to be clearly defined in terms of the informational priorities of the intranet, and the influence of content creators needs to be defined in terms of user expectations and perspectives. This will enable strategic objectives to be translated into concrete objectives that fulfil user needs.

User-centric design

Rather like businesses that insist their employees are their most important resource while neglecting good employment practice, many intranets are claimed to address users while overlooking user needs in favour of corporate objectives. It is not in itself advantageous to the user for an organisation to slash its print costs by publishing internal material on the intranet, especially if they then have to spend the time printing out the information.

User-centric design means prioritising the user perspective over that of other groups, essentially inverting the management pyramid shown in Figure 3.1. This means taking a bottom-up approach to designing an intranet, starting with user needs, working up through content creator needs and skills, up through intranet management, to arrive at strategic management and objectives. Strategic objectives, both for the intranet as a whole and for intranet content, must be defined around user perspectives, needs and behaviour.

The first stage in this process involves clearly identifying user needs, and providing processes by which those needs can be transformed into working information structures. This must occur on a structural level; paying lip-service to user centric design is not enough. Similarly, imposing the prioritisation of the user perspectives on management frameworks that have been created in order to underline the role of managers will not work. An overhaul of the relationship between users, content creators and managers is necessary to enable user-centric design to take place. The process of implementing this is the subject of Chapter 4.

The role of the information professional

Information professionals can have an important role in bridging the gaps in expectation between different user groups and between interested parties. Because of their understanding of how the characteristics of information can influence the use and management of information, they are ideally suited to determining strategy based around users.

Intranets are not IT applications. They rely on technology, but they are not driven by technology. They are driven by the desire to inform, the need underpinning the economies of the developed world to locate, process and distribute information. They are *information* tools, and should be managed as collections of information, not as technological solutions. The benchmarks for all content should always be not only that it *informs*, but also that it informs in a way that is either more efficient or cheaper than alternative resources. Because information professionals understand those alternative resources, they are better placed to make these judgements.

Intranets should be problem-led, rather than solution-led. In other words, they should tackle existing problems in the provision and management of information resources within organisations. Much of the competition over ownership of information can arise because new solutions are applied where there are no existing problems; existing resources that have served the needs of users and groups within the organisation perfectly well are very often replaced by solutions that do not, or which aim to make the jobs of everyone easier at the expense of the jobs of a few. This can cause real anxiety in the implementation of intranets. Because information professionals understand information, because their priority is the management of information rather than the management of technology, and because they are far more likely to understand the existing problems in information provision and management within the organisation, their role in intranet implementation is vital. Intranet projects that are driven from an IT or technological perspective will fail, because they may introduce as many new problems as they resolve. Intranets need to be created as information resources, from an understanding of what information is, how it functions within the organisation and what issues there are with existing provision.

Summary

This chapter has examined how strategic objectives can translate into concrete objectives that fail to meet the needs of users. This occurs because at each stage of the management process, there is a translation of objectives not in terms of user needs but in terms of provider needs. Overcoming this tendency is dependent on prioritising user perspectives in defining roles and responsibilities.

Part 2
Designing intranets

Models of intranet design can be divided into three types:

- those based on interaction
- those based on management processes
- those based on business processes.

These varying perspectives are cumulative; each type of model contributes to the understanding gained from the others.

Interaction-based models

In her 1998 book, *The 21st Century Intranet*, Jennifer Stone Gonzales approaches intranet architecture by modelling the kinds of interaction through which users engage with intranets. She identifies four types of intranet from the kind of technology that each uses and the type of function it serves:

1. *The publication model* – consisting of one-way static communication and relying predominantly on pure HTML. The function it serves is to disseminate information and documents.

2. *The asymmetrical interaction model* – consisting of two-way, time-delayed communication to disseminate information and documents in the same way as the publication model, but also allowing feedback in the form of web forms or e-mail links.

3. *The symmetrical interaction model* – consisting of multidirectional communication that allows not only the dissemination of information and documents but also asynchronous communication in the form of intranet discussion groups etc.

4. *The synchronous virtual environment model* – consisting of real-time, dynamic, multidirectional communication in the form of video-conferencing, speech recognition and voice e-mail.

In real-world implementations, this model may in some respects be regarded as aspirational, outlining potential stages of intranet development that may not be realistic within a given organisation at a given time, nor necessarily suited to an organisation's needs.

Management-based models

A second way of approaching intranet architecture is to model the kinds of management structures that control the creation and ordering of information. For example, Gupta and Wachter (1997) identified four models for managing intranets:

1. *The decentralised model* – where contributors of intranet content are free to publish any information they deem appropriate.

2. *The centralised model* – where policies and procedures for intranet management are formulated and implemented to control development.

3. *The mixed model* – where policies and procedures are drawn up and passed down through an organisation but where the contributors have responsibility to publish within these policies and procedures with little or no centralised control.

4. *The support-services model* – where the organisation provides support for intranet contributors through the development process

Wilkinson, Charlton and Sice (2000) have presented a similar model based on decentralised, federal, corporate services and federal bureau approaches.

Business process-based models

A third model focuses not on how the technology of intranets works, how they are managed or the modes by which people interact with them, but on what we expect users to achieve using the intranet. This is not the same question as what we want the intranet to achieve, which may be characterised broadly as *generating a cost reduction* or *achieving an efficiency gain*. The question is simpler: what problems do we want the intranet to solve? Intranets can resemble solutions looking for a problem, rather than tools that are specifically targeted to address identifiable needs.

This approach models intranet design on business processes, concentrating on the way in which the intranet serves various functions within an organisation and facilitates the processes within that organisation. In this type of model, the intranet forms only a part of a wider information and communications strategy.

Elements of intranet design

The different approaches highlight three issues:

- the kind of technological basis on which intranets are built;
- the kind of managerial relationship that exists between content creators and intranet managers;
- the kind of information processes that intranets deliver.

Although the models are in themselves useful in understanding the role of intranets within the organisation, none is sufficient to enable us to build a managed intranet from the bottom up. The issues they highlight are interrelated and each issue has knock-on effects on the others.

In examining the issues involved in designing workable intranets in Part 2 of this book, some of the layered hierarchies of which intranets consist are deconstructed, and how to make each function effectively is explored. What works for users very often does not work for content creators, what works for content creators very often does not work for intranet managers and what works for intranet managers very often does not work for IT professionals. Intranets are frequently built to reflect the concerns of one or other of these interested parties, or to reflect the needs of specific groups of users within the organisation. In Part 2 how to design intranets that work for everybody is explored.

4

Elements of intranet architecture

Aims

This chapter explores the role of information architecture and organisation in the design of intranets. It begins by examining the different ways in which intranet design can be discussed, in terms of their physical, content management and logical structures. Each is important in designing and implementing successful intranets, or in revamping unsuccessful intranets. The chapter also explores the different types of hierarchy that may be involved in organising the logical structure of an intranet, from departmental hierarchies, through format-orientated hierarchies, to process-orientated hierarchies, and how each of these impact on the usability of intranets for different information needs.

The chapter then discusses the role of metadata and taxonomies in intranet design, and finally ways of releasing intranets from the bonds of formal navigation structures.

Physical structure of intranets

The physical structure of an intranet consists of the wires and servers that constitute the physical network on which the intranet is housed. A successful intranet can be designed around high-capacity servers and networks, or dial-up networking and basic servers. Intranets are not primarily technological solutions and therefore a basic physical structure will still yield good returns if it is well managed. Beyond the basic function of enabling communication between computers, the physical architecture is therefore the least important element in creating a successful intranet. However, the physical structure of an intranet will influence intranet content management strategies by determining two qualities of that content:

- the kinds of applications that the intranet is able to carry;
- the currency of the content on that intranet.

Within a small, single-site organisation, an intranet may function using a single server, or a collection of servers managing unique tasks. The servers will essentially be on-line at all times and their content able to be updated in real time. Information should become available throughout the organisation as it is uploaded onto the server. Bandwidth on a network within a single-site organisation is unlikely to be a significant issue, although the available bandwidth may limit data-intensive applications such as video-conferencing. An illustration of this kind of structure is given in Figure 4.1. This is the optimum set-up for an intranet. However, such a design is not usually possible in multi-site organisations with distributed networks. There are likely to be practical restrictions on traffic volumes across distributed networks, because transmitting data between geographically dispersed sites is more expensive than transmitting data on local area networks. This will influence the viability of different kinds of resource. Furthermore, the available bandwidth may vary from site to site, with large-capacity fixed lines forming the

Figure 4.1 Single-server structure

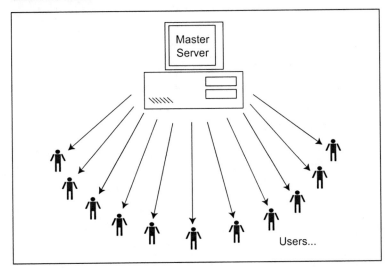

backbone of a wide area network and smaller-capacity lines serving far-flung or underdeveloped locations.

There are three options for implementing an intranet over a distributed network of this kind. The first is to maintain a single server, or a collection of servers managing unique tasks, which all users access across the wide area network regardless of their location, as above. The key advantages of this approach are:

- information is accessed and updated in real-time;

- all employees access a single version of the intranet;

- hardware and maintenance costs are low.

The main disadvantage is the extra load carried on the wide area network, the majority of which will not be used for information that needs to be updated in real time. For example, a staff telephone directory in practical terms does not need to be updated on a minute-by-minute basis, and therefore there is no real need for the data to be resubmitted to a distant location every time it is requested by a user. The IT architecture of such a system will be limited in its capacity for future growth. If the organisation expands significantly, the loads placed on the server will grow comparatively, and over time the performance of the intranet will deteriorate. In these circumstances, speed of transmission of data across the network may become an issue, especially for locations that are less well served by the network. This may generate 'patchy' intranet performance.

The second solution is a distributed intranet consisting of a master server duplicated periodically to site servers in individual locations (Figure 4.2). A user in any given location accesses the intranet as a resource housed locally and updated regularly over the wide area network. Content creators publish their updates to the master server, and a schedule of replication occurs to duplicate the information around the local intranet servers. The advantages of such an implementation are:

- a reduction in data loads across the wide area network;
- an increase in speed of data transmission to the end user;
- an increase in the data capacity of the intranet.

The disadvantage of this model is that the intranet cannot be updated in real time. The master server would be scheduled to duplicate the data periodically – perhaps overnight or at weekends when demands on the wide area network are lighter. For the majority of applications, this may not be a significant disadvantage; however, such an approach will affect the use of the intranet as a communications tool. Organisation-wide intranet-based discussions, for example, would not be possible.

A third approach that in principle should have the advantages of both models but with none of the disadvantages is the mixed model. The core of the intranet is carried on a

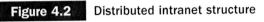

Figure 4.2   Distributed intranet structure

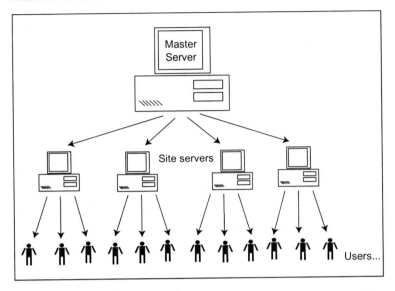

distributed network of servers that are duplicates of a master server, and each is accessed locally in each location, as in Figure 4.2. Information on the intranet that need not be updated in real time is therefore accessed locally, reducing the duplication of low-priority traffic across the network. However, for real-time applications, a parallel 'live' server is maintained centrally, which users access across the network, as in Figure 4.1. There is one fundamental disadvantage to this approach: the complexity involved in integrating and managing it.

The physical architecture of an intranet may ultimately be out of your control. However, it will significantly affect the types of applications that you are able to implement, and the management processes that will be required to maintain them. For a single-site organisation, the single server approach is preferable; for multi-site organisations the mixed-model approach will usually offer the greatest flexibility, prevailing network conditions permitting.

Whichever solution is adopted, you must be clear which it is *before* you begin working on the information architecture and intranet design. There is little point planning intranet discussion groups if each posting takes a day or a week to be duplicated around the organisation on a distributed-intranet, and there is no point in planning perhaps expensive data-intensive applications such as proprietary database-driven content if the network cannot handle the data loads.

Content management structure

The content management structure of an intranet is the way in which information is grouped to maximise the efficiency and ease of updating that content. This must be designed-in; it will not occur organically from the process of recruiting content creators. We have seen in Part 1 that content creators and content-area managers may have specific objectives and perspectives defining their approach to the provision of information across the intranet that conflict with the objectives and perspectives of others. These competing perspectives must be reconciled.

There are two ways of arranging a content management structure:

1. centralised content creation within a team whose primary responsibility is for intranet content creation;

2. distributed content creation, with key individuals within departments, offices or sections taking over responsibility for creating content.

The centralised approach encourages the content creation process to focus on the specific goals or objectives of the intranet, making it easier to maintain consistency and reliability of content, and easier to create efficient information architecture. However, as an intranet grows, the volume of content centralised content creation teams are required to create may quickly become overwhelming, and this will act as a limiting factor on the future growth and ultimate effectiveness of the intranet. Content creation also becomes detached from the expertise within the organisation, and can become detached from user needs. The content creators rely on others, either users or information specialists, to inform them of information needs. Because of this, many intranets that began as centrally produced resources quickly moved to a distributed content creation model, and distributed creation of content has become the norm. However, for smaller organisations, or deliberately restricted intranets, centralised creation of content may be ideal.

The distributed approach maintains content creation at the coalface of an organisation. Content is created within the departments or groups that actually use the information and should therefore reflect actual information needs. Areas of content may consist of individual pages, or of sophisticated collections of information and resources such as departmental sites, but are likely to consist of a combination of the two. Although the advantages of this approach are clear, the disadvantages are many, not least the difficulty in managing consistency, quality and currency of information.

Logical structure

The logical structure of an intranet is that which users experience when they navigate through it. This may not relate directly to the navigation structure itself, as we will see. Because the logical structure of an intranet is married to its usability, we should pay a good deal of attention to its functionality. Logical structures of intranets often mirror their content management structures, forcing users to navigate through an intranet that is organised in a way that is most convenient for the updating and maintenance of content, not for locating it. This is always a mistake. The logical structure should be for the benefit of the user, not the content manager.

There is no reason for the logical and content management structures of an intranet to be co-dependent. The logical structure should reflect the ways in which people use the intranet; in other words, it should be designed around user behaviour. We have seen in Part 1 how users and content creators often have a very different relationship with the information that is held on an intranet.

As a user clicks on a hyperlink within the logical structure, they are stepping down one level in the hierarchy of that structure. This hierarchy can either be shallow or deep: it can either have many branches but few levels, or many levels but few branches. Examples of shallow and deep hierarchies are shown in Figures 4.3 and 4.4.

Shallow hierarchies have the following characteristics:

- a greater range of information about available content is presented to the user at any one time;
- the user is required to progress through fewer levels of the hierarchy to reach the information they need.

Conversely, deep hierarchies have the following characteristics:

- users are better guided to the information they need;
- users are required to make simpler choices in navigating the intranet.

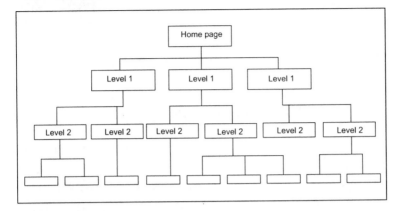

Figure 4.3 Example of a deep hierarchy

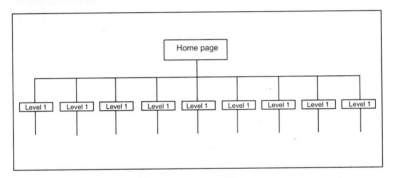

Figure 4.4 Example of a shallow hierarchy

Studies have shown that in web usage, the amount of links a user is required to follow in order to reach the information they need is critical to the likelihood of them persevering with the task (Nielsen, 2000). However, with intranets the situation is complicated by the users' greater familiarity with the information for which they are looking and by their greater experience of the resource, so there is no reason to assume this rule of thumb necessarily holds true. Learning the layout of shallow hierarchies is a more time-consuming task than learning the layout of deep hierarchies, as the latter have inherently less structure. However, some people prefer to have a greater range of information available in fewer clicks. Generally, there should be a preference for shallow hierarchical design in intranet navigation structures, but it need not be an either/or decision, as we shall see.

Navigation hierarchies

The choices with which users are presented in their navigation of an intranet should not be derived from content management processes – in other words, derived from departmental *responsibility* for the information they seek – but should be based on the function of the information for the user. Even if the intranet is arranged into discrete content areas or 'sites' that are the specific responsibility of individual groups within the organisation, there is no need to force this perspective on the user. The types of navigational hierarchies that can be developed fall into three categories: organisation-orientated hierarchies, information-orientated hierarchies and process-orientated hierarchies.

Organisation-orientated hierarchies

Intranet navigation can be arranged around the existing structures of an organisation: the departments, sites, offices, groups, etc. For example, individual pages can be grouped into content areas that reflect the concerns of departments within the organisation, and labelled appropriately. Such an approach will mirror the content management structure of the intranet, although not necessarily exclusively. The hierarchy can be deepened by grouping departments together under broader headings, or made shallower by breaking off parts of departments into discrete content areas.

An intranet that from a user's point of view echoes the departmental structures of the organisation has the advantage of familiarity. The users should be able to understand the logic informing the classification with which they are presented. For the intranet manager, a logical structure that reflects the content management structure of the intranet will make the task of implementing and managing it easier. However, the level of familiarity with the organisation required to be able to use the navigation effectively might be beyond that which may be reasonably expected of any individual user. The tendency that we saw in Part 1 for users naturally to become most familiar with those content areas that they use most frequently is exacerbated by this kind of navigation, which discourages use outside of those content areas.

Another disadvantage of such an approach is that it can introduce a conflict of expectation about the context in which any given piece of information belongs. For example, a user may have an expectation that subject-related information on a university intranet be located on the departmental site, when because of the allocation of responsibility for creating the content it is actually available on the library services site.

A further weakness in a logical structure that is based on the organisation's own structure is that the same information can logically belong in several different locations. For example, client-facing departments within an organisation may have a need for standard client letters, implying that these letters should be available from each content area. Similarly, each department may have its own records of employee specialisms. The logic behind an intranet structured along content management lines implies that single resources, be they client letters or employee skills information, are split across many branches of the structural hierarchy.

Similarly, information that is used in one department may logically belong under the content area of another department or section, because that other department or section produces or manages it. In a logical structure that reflects the organisation's own internal structure, the format of information and the use to which it is put is less important in determining its location than who 'owns' or manages it. Because users faced with this approach are encouraged to view the intranet as a collection of discrete interest groups, they are discouraged from using information across its breadth. The structure encourages them to identify with a single part of the intranet. It entrenches the departmental division of information.

An organisation-orientated logical structure is most suited to disseminating information concerning the organisation itself – for fulfilling the communication or knowledge management functions of an intranet as discussed in Part 1.

Information-orientated navigation hierarchies

Content may also be grouped by its type or format. For example, forms for internal use may be grouped under a single content area, forms for external use under another, letters under a third, policy documents under a fourth, marketing strategies under a fifth, and so on.

The user navigating such a hierarchy is presented with a different set of choices than when navigating an organisation-orientated hierarchy. Where before they would be obliged to consider which department is responsible for the information they need, now they must consider what *kind* of information it is that they need. This produces a closer alignment between the choices they make in their navigation and the actual use to which they will put the information they require. For example, a user looking for a standard letter to send to a client need no longer first have to make a judgement about which group within the organisation is likely to be responsible for the letter, but need only identify what type of letter they are seeking.

Information-orientated navigation hierarchies can be difficult to manage within the context of competing expectations. In order to make them work seamlessly, there needs to be a high degree of standardisation in style and design of content, together with content management procedures that allow information to be managed on a page-by-page basis. Such an approach could be implemented by centralising the authorship of all navigation levels except those containing actual content – in other words by bringing the entire hierarchical structure under centralised control. However, this is likely to constrict an intranet within a planned taxonomy that may inhibit its development.

Process-orientated navigation hierarchies

Process-orientated navigation hierarchies are built from the tasks that users perform. The logical structure of the intranet groups content by the use to which it will be put by the user, rather than by the form of the information or who is responsible for it. For example, all the information involved in the process of starting employment, from the forms required, the policy documents that need to be reviewed, to information about corporate structure and strategy, can be grouped together under a single heading. Similarly, all the information involved in everyday tasks, such as pitching to clients, bidding for research funding or handling expense claims, can be grouped under single headings.

Unlike information-orientated hierarchies and organisation-orientated hierarchies, the information under a process-orientated hierarchy need not logically belong in one location. Individual pieces of information may appear in several places under the hierarchy as it is collected together and recollected for different processes. The information remains unique, but becomes accessible by multiple pathways.

Process-orientated hierarchies have the advantage of mirroring the work processes within an organisation. This aligns the decisions that users make in their navigation of the Web with the tasks they are trying to perform. However, within organisations there are no ends to the unique tasks that could possibly be contained within a process-orientated hierarchy. There would need to be a good deal of selection from those possible processes, and thus the hierarchy will never become truly comprehensive. Although process-orientated hierarchies are a useful way of approaching navigation, it is unlikely that they can fulfil the function of a sole navigation solution.

Parallel and multiple hierarchies

Most intranet navigation structures are organised largely on the basis of the underlying content management structure. In other words, the navigational choices presented to the user reflect the way in which responsibility for content areas has been distributed among individuals or groups within the organisation. The predominant cause of this is the ease with which such a hierarchy can be implemented and maintained. Interested groups need merely be identified, and responsibility for creating content delegated appropriately. However, such an approach does not facilitate use of the intranet, because the structure reflects the needs of content creators not of users.

Many intranets offer the user a single navigational hierarchy, with perhaps the support of some additional navigational aids such as quick links and bookmarks. Some intra-nets will refine the user-view of this hierarchy using pushed and personalised content, but the underlying hierarchy remains in place.

A principle of classification is that every piece of information should fit into one and only one place within a classification scheme. With physical resources, such as books, this reduces duplication of resources and facilitates version management. However, intranets do not contain physical resources, and navigation hierarchies are not physical classification schemes. It is possible for one piece of information to be located in several different places under an intranet navigation structure, because that structure merely points to the information, it does not define it. It is a logical structure: the way in which the user locates information. It is not the basis on which that information need be managed, nor produced. Just as libraries have shelf numbers and catalogue entries for each item, intranets can house multiple pathways to information without duplicating that information.

The navigation hierarchies above have been presented as if they are mutually exclusive. However, a more successful way of approaching navigation is to implement concurrent multiple hierarchies providing multiple pathways to the same information. Using this approach, the integrity of a departmental site can be maintained while the same information is repackaged as part of either a process-orientated structure or an information-orientated structure. The same piece of information, for example an expenses form, can appear under the finance department content area in an organisation-orientated hierarchy, under an internal forms content area in an information-orientated hierarchy and under as many process content areas under a process-orientated hierarchy as there are processes in the organisation in which it is required.

This use of multiple hierarchies enables users to adopt the most appropriate navigation mode for their objectives. When they are using content that is familiar to them, content that is essential to their role in the organisation, they will use the structures they are most familiar with and which most represents their role – their departmental site. However, when they are looking for less familiar information that can be identified by type – be it a form, a policy document or a standard letter – they can switch navigational modes to search using information-orientated hierarchies. When they are following specific information-intensive tasks, such as progressing through an induction programme, they can switch to process-orientated hierarchies. The user may not recognise the difference between these three approaches, because they mirror the way we think about information under different circumstances. They will switch modes automatically as they make a decision about which of the specific links with which they are presented is most likely to lead to the information they require. A typical home page, for example, may ask the user to select 'departments', 'materials' or 'job packs', listing the various second-level options below each. It is not made explicit that they are being channelled into different structures; they will simply follow what seems the best option.

Users are no longer required to have a good understanding of how the intranet is structured, because the intranet is now flexibly structured around their changing relationship to content. An intranet using this model ceases to be merely a collection of sites and becomes a collection of information. From the users' perspective, the HTML becomes the managed unit of information, liberated from the ownership of individuals or groups within the organisation.

There are two ways to implement such an approach. The first is a managerial approach, requiring nothing more than an HTML editor and planning. The second is a technological approach, requiring the implementation of a complete intranet metadata content-set and taxonomy, combined with a database-powered intranet produced with a sophisticated content management system. Both will work, but the technological approach is necessarily more powerful. The managerial approach uses pathway editors.

Pathway editors

Pathway editors are individuals who are responsible not for creating content or for managing content creation and updating, but simply for repackaging existing intranet content for new contexts. This may be in the form of new hierarchies, or of meta-pages that act as subject gateways to information on an intranet. In order to make the role of pathway editor possible, there are two requirements:

- A consistent design applied to intranet content, preferably with the use of full HTML encoding and cascading style sheets. This will enable individual pages to be repackaged for their new context. At the very least, consistent design will create the illusion that the information has been especially created for its new context.

- Uniformity in the way in which individual pages are managed – the file names they are given, the directory structures they fall under and the circumstances under which these characteristics are changed. As much care and attention must be paid to the file organisation of intranet content as to the pre-existing navigation organisation. This will require content to be managed through its life cycle in a consistent way.

Ensuring these elements are in place should make the pathway editor's task straightforward. Pathway editors merely gather together information held on the intranet in new collections, either by producing meta-pages of links, or by embedding that information within new contexts using a database-driven content management system, or even using frames.

Metadata and taxonomies

Metadata is data about data. A library catalogue entry is a piece of metadata – data about a book. In intranet terms, metadata are data about intranet content. These data should be developed at the level of individual units of content, which for practical terms can be regarded as the page. With traditional content stored as individual HTML files, there are two approaches to storing metadata about intranet content:

- store the metadata *with* the content, as a header to the HTML file;

- store the data *apart* from the content, in a metadata database.

The advantages of the first approach include the ease of implementation and robustness of maintaining metadata with content. As content is deleted, the associated metadata is also deleted. A good search engine will index the metadata, and should allow flexibility in the exploitation of these data in the weighting of search results. Implementing the second approach is more problematic, but has the advantage of divorcing metadata creation from content creation. It will also give greater flexibility in manipulating the metadata. In content management systems metadata may be stored with the content, as individual fields within the database record. This allows not only ease of management of these data, but also greater flexibility in their use.

Metadata comes in two basic types:

- that which aids the management of content;
- that which aids the retrieval of content.

The first type might include such data as the date of creation of the page, the date of redundancy or a review period. The second type of metadata is descriptive of content. Descriptive metadata *describes* the information to which it relates just like a catalogue record, and this may be in terms of its subject matter, currency, form or any other quality that may be important. This second type of metadata can be used to cluster content together into classes of information, which can subsequently be manipulated, for example by being pushed out to individual users who have declared an interest in a given type of information.

Because it describes information, metadata can be used to determine the usefulness of that information for any given purpose, and because metadata can be implemented using taxonomies, it can be used to automate those processes. Information can be resorted and sifted to fit the precise demands of any given situation.

Navigation structures, the logical structure of the intranet and the shape of the intranet that confronts the user can be constructed by manual encoding. However, by using taxonomies and metadata, the location of any given piece of information within each of these structures can be defined precisely in relation to the qualities of that information as it is produced or prepared, and *automatically* slotted into the navigation hierarchies on the fly depending on these definitions. The content management system will essentially resort its content database by these structural fields to generate dynamic content and navigational aids.

Implementing this in a sophisticated way relies not so much on technological solutions as on robust taxonomies to define and classify information.

Building taxonomies that work

We have already seen one kind of taxonomy in relation to intranet design: the navigation schemes that give an intranet a logical structure. Taxonomies for metadata work using the same principles.

Traditional information taxonomies are based on the principle that one unit of information need be ordered within a structured schema of all the available information. In library terms, this relates to an item on the shelf, whether that item is a monograph, a series or a piece of audio-visual media. The important principle observed is that wherever the unit of information is scheduled to be placed, it should be placed only there, and not elsewhere either concurrently or sequentially. It should not move from its allotted space in the taxonomy, nor should it occupy more than one space.

This traditional method of developing taxonomies grew out of the need to manage information as a manifest physical entity, such as a book. These entities, inherently unique, need to be ordered by their relationship with each other. Thus books are placed on the shelf in relation to their subject matter, and because an individual book cannot occupy more than one space at a time, its subject matter needs to be defined in terms of its predominant subject classification. It does not matter how many subject areas an individual unit of information such as a book meanders through; once the predominant subject classification has been determined, that is where the book will sit. Traditional classification schemes therefore have the effect of compartmentalising knowledge into neat little blocks into which information can be slotted. An artificial order is imposed upon that knowledge, an order that allows us to navigate easily and successfully through that knowledge, but which obscures many of the semantic and associative relationships between disparate parts.

Traditional subject classification is one dimensional in nature – all information is placed somewhere on one long exhaustive line of all the knowledge subject areas available. New knowledge is classified by increasing the granularity within that dimension – by breaking up existing subject classes into subclasses. However, with intranets the same units of information can be accessed by many different pathways, combined and recombined to generate new resources with new contextual meaning. Our metadata taxonomies therefore need to be more flexible than traditional classification.

Faceted classification

Faceted classification is multi-dimensional by nature. A given subject area is broken down into facets, each of which represents one aspect of that subject area, and each of these facets is itself given limited classes. For example, people can be classified by the facets of gender, nationality and age. For any individual, terms are selected from a restricted set for each facet, which combine to create a multi-dimensional classification. Faceted classification has become popular with web developers as it better reflects the uncertain, and to some extent unordered, terrain of the Internet.

By utilising this ability of faceted classification to define qualities of information, we can begin to build up our intranet taxonomy. For example, using the organisation-orientated, information-orientated and process-orientated structures presented above, we could define three facets, one for each. We may define, for example, each of our organisation's departments or sections under the organisation-orientated facet, define each class or type of information under our information-orientated facet and each business process in which information may be used under our process-orientated facet. Each facet is a piece of metadata. Each page would be defined by metadata that consisted of three facets: its organisation-orientated definition its information-orientated definition and its process-orientated definition. For example, an expenses form could be defined in metadata as belonging to the finance department, being an internal form and used in expense claims. By doing this, we have already built up a relatively sophisticated approach.

However, this is not a true hierarchy; there are no nested levels of terms arranged in a hierarchical relationship. There are in fact only two levels, the facets and the terms defined within them. Thus, although this kind of metadata may be useful in information retrieval via searches, it is unlikely to be a great deal of use in arranging the navigation structure of an intranet. To do this, we need to go a stage further, and turn our faceted taxonomy into an information thesaurus.

Information thesauri

Thesauri, like navigation schemes, are hierarchical structures for information organisation and retrieval. In a thesaurus, a parent term will enclose a cluster of subordinate terms, and each of these subordinate terms will itself be the parent of another cluster of subordinate terms, and so on through the scheme. The result is a tree-like structure that mirrors that of the navigation schemes shown in Figures 4.3 and 4.4, with one exception: in a traditional information-retrieval thesaurus there will be many starting points, whereas in an intranet navigation scheme there is usually only one: the home page.

Aspects of metadata should therefore be conceived in terms of taxonomies built on the principles of thesauri construction. There is insufficient space here to go into detail about the process of generating a taxonomy, except to say that the only practical way to control terms is to centralise the control of metadata. This can be achieved by building the taxonomy into the meta-tagging process – whether that process is performed centrally or dispersed across content creators – but allowing sufficient flexibility and feedback mechanisms for that taxonomy to be expanded as required. Leaving it where we are will enable powerful pushed-content applications to be introduced, and should allow the classification of information with a relative degree of precision.

Intranets unbound

Yet need we leave it here? Can we make classifying information on intranets as fuzzy as the hyperlinks that create associations between pages? Can we make metadata form around the associative and semantic connections that form the basis of hypertext?

Thesauri depend on the principle that each term belongs in only one place in the tree-like structure, under only one grandparent, one great-grandparent and one great-great-grandparent term. They have an application in the development of taxonomies for intranet content precisely because they mirror the tree-like hierarchies of intranet navigation schemes, allowing the navigation options available to individual users to be generated in real-time. However, they differ from those schemes by fixing the relationships between individual terms – slotting all information into its appropriate box. As we have seen, there is no real reason for this restriction on intranets; these classification methods are optimised for circumstances in which there are real limitations on the organisation of information – for example library shelves.

When Tim Berners-Lee invented the Web, it was the mould of these rigid structures that he was attempting to break. He was trying to create a system that would allow information stored on computers to be located by means of semantic and associative connections generated by humans who understand the relationship between disparate pieces of information. In doing so, he was attempting to mimic the way in which the brain stores and sorts information.

Intranets should be designed as fuzzy networks of information, networks where the precise relationship between individual pieces of information is not defined until it is needed, and shifts over time with the changing contexts for which it is required. Strictly hierarchical relationships do not allow this. The horizontal hyperlinks between the information on each level of an intranet hierarchy encourage the creation of semantic and associative connections, and it is therefore important to promote these horizontal hyperlinks. However, this alone is not enough to create a truly fuzzy network, because as we have seen content creators are always more likely to link to information within their site than outside of it. To create a truly fuzzy intranet we need to use spiral classification schemes.

Spiral classification is based on the broad concept of information thesauri. Each term within the scheme has a parent, synonyms and children. But unlike ordinary faceted classification, each term can have more that one parent. It can appear in more than one place in the scheme. As a consequence, terms can become parents of their own grandparents; children of their own grandchildren. That bugbear of classifiers and computer programmers alike is set free: loops (just as it is set free by HTML itself). Consequently, users following a navigation scheme built on this principle can spiral through information in the classification, tumbling through the information field rather than down it. This is the same principle on which normal hyperlinks are constructed, but with two important differences.

First, spiral schemes are ordered along regular lines. Each term has a shifting relationship to other terms, but those other terms spiral around it while the term itself is fixed. Each page has a shifting relationship to other pages; while the user is viewing the page it is fixed, but becomes the launch pad for a thousand other enquiries. The classification scheme works using regular rules for classifying information. Second, following the principles of true hypertext, implementing a spiral classification scheme allows users to return along the same hyperlinks they arrived on, allows them to trace their way back along the pathways they used to find the page they were on. Spiral pathways follow the principle of the Web itself, offering an infinite number of routes to any single page, which are robust and able to withstand the changing information landscape brought about by adding and removing information.

Spiral navigation tools can be implemented on an intranet in the form of footnotes to each page, giving links to parent pages and dependent pages. The metadata can be generated by meta-tagging pages, or by automatically generating a spiral classification from the hyperlinks that already exist on the intranet. Both approaches utilise the associative and semantic processing of humans to relate pieces of information, and both processes perform this in relation to the qualities of information itself, rather than an abstract scheme.

The meta-tagging approach implies that content creators navigate through the classification terms using those same semantic and associative connections, and selecting the most appropriate terms. Because the network is fuzzy, it is extremely robust to imprecision or inadvertent introduction of synonyms. With relatively little control, inexperienced classifiers will be able not only to classify within the scheme accurately but also to introduce new terms that will themselves over time filter to their correct semantic or associative positions. Terms are simply defined in relation to their dependent terms, not their parent terms, with the simple rule that any term cannot be its own dependent. Unique IDs in a database containing the term index will reference other unique IDs identifying them as dependents.

Navigation aids can be built on the principle of spiral classification, such that users can navigate parallel to the intranet through the term index until they find the term they require and then retrieve all the pages so indexed. Users can participate in the construction of the relationships, and their maintenance, by using voting buttons, or usage analysis to ascertain statistically how accurate any single relationship between any two terms within the spiral scheme is. The more it is used, the more accurate it will become, and the more it will reflect users' expectations of where hyperlinks will lead.

Over time, the fuzzy network will evolve sufficiently that hyperlinks within textual information can be automatically generated depending upon the semantic and associative connections identified by the spiral classification scheme. The navigation scheme will build itself. The index will build itself. More importantly, so will those semantic and associative connections that constitute fuzzy networks.

Summary

This chapter has explored the various types of structure that underlie intranets: the physical structure of the network and servers, the managerial structure of content management and the logical structure of navigation hierarchies. Different types of physical structure change the kinds of resources that are viable on an intranet. The content management structure will define who is responsible for each piece of content. There is no reason why this arrangement of responsibilities for content creation need be imposed on the user as a navigation scheme, although it may help orientate the user within the navigation structure. Navigation structures should also incorporate consideration of the type of information and its function within business processes.

5

A step-by-step guide
to implementing intranets

Aims

This chapter outlines the process of implementing a new intranet, or of revamping an existing intranet. A traditional project management approach might label the phases involved *planning*, *implementation* and *review*. This chapter will cover the first two of these stages. Chapter 6 concentrates on the third stage: review or, in the case of intranets, ongoing management. Once an intranet has been launched, it moves into a phase of continued re-evaluation and development.

Both chapters concentrate on the information management aspects of an intranet project. Other issues that are outside the scope of this book should also be taken into account, such as promotion, marketing and training. The planning and implementation phases are divided here into 11 steps:

Step 1:   Setting management priorities

Step 2:   Defining strategic objectives

Step 3:   Assessing information needs

Step 4:   Organising content areas

Step 5:   Identifying teams

Step 6:   Design, style and policy

Step 7:   Information architecture

Step 8:   Selecting pathway editors

Step 9:   Centrally managed resources

Step 10:   Piloting, previewing and reviewing

Step 11:   Rolling out the intranet.

A flowchart at the end of this chapter summarises all these stages.

Step 1: Setting management priorities

The first step in implementing and managing a successful intranet is deciding what it is you are managing. There are as many answers to this question as there are intranets, but they fall into four distinct categories: technology, communication, information and people. Predominantly this is the order in which the management priorities for intranets are set. Technological innovation generates capabilities for communication of intellectual capital and information, associated around the work of people. Intranets are viewed as technological solutions to communications and information needs.

This is precisely the wrong view to take. The most important priority for managing intranets is managing the people involved: their roles and their relationship with the intranet, be they intranet managers, content creators or end-users. Part 1 has examined how individual outlooks and roles can affect intranet implementation, and should be read in conjunction with this stage. The second most important priority for managing intranets is information architecture, which includes managing content areas and their coverage, central information resources, and the navigation and meta-data structures that bind them together. Chapter 4 focuses on these aspects of information management, and should be read in conjunction with this stage. The third priority is communication, not only communication processes but also the way that the intranet is promoted. Technology is the final aspect. Intranets can succeed or fail with either sophisticated or unsophisticated technological solutions.

When revamping an existing intranet, a shift may be required from understanding the intranet as a solution driven by technology to understanding it as a solution driven by people. Technology exists not for its own sake but to make tasks easier. Chapter 6 discusses this in more detail.

Step 2: Defining strategic objectives

Once the management priorities have been accepted and adopted, the strategic objectives of an intranet must be defined. The four functions of intranets are discussed in Chapter 2 (information dissemination, information storage, communication and knowledge management), and should be read in conjunction with this stage.

Objectives for an intranet should be defined in the context of a broader information and communications policy. Choosing objectives across information systems and media is a matter of selecting the best solution to any given problem. The intranet should not be established in competition with other information and communications systems and media by defining its objectives too widely, but should operate in collaboration with those other systems and media. Comprehensive coverage should be provided *between* alternative approaches. For example, e-mail is more suitable than an intranet for some communication functions because of its immediacy and the reasonable assurance that a communicated message will be received. Demarcate what kinds of communications are going to be delivered using each communications medium.

With every decision the scope of the intranet should be narrowed. The less it does, the more effectively it will do it. The less an intranet is viewed as a generic solution, the more effective it will become as an information tool for targeted information retrieval (see Chapter 1). Avoid turning your intranet into an information dumping ground by setting clear and realistic objectives to delimit the extent of the role it will play. These limited objectives should be defined at the outset. When in doubt, leave it out – the role of the intranet can be expanded at a later stage, if absolutely necessary. Initially it is important to be confident not only that the objectives you set can be achieved, but also that they can be *best* achieved using an intranet. This will determine a clear strategy for success.

The precise objective set will depend on the context of your organisation. When setting generic objectives, such as improving communications, you should list the concrete solutions that will be implemented on an intranet to achieve the generic objective. When setting out multiple objectives, always prioritise them. For example, make it clear that the first job of your intranet is to disseminate information, the second job to store information, etc. It is likely that you will want to limit the objectives to only two or three of the four functions discussed in Chapter 2, in order to maintain focus. Keep in mind the discussion of the limitations of intranets.

Step 3: Assessing information needs

The next stage is to match information needs against the objectives for your intranet by conducting an information needs assessment. This may result in an adjustment to the objectives of both an intranet and a wider information and communications policy. However, the information needs assessment must come *after* setting objectives, because those objectives will in part define the conduct of the information needs assessment. The process of assessing information needs itself is outside the scope of this book, but there is much useful literature on the subject (for example, see Nicholas, 1996).

From the information needs determined in this process, which of them the intranet can realistically fulfil needs to be decided. It is better to do well half of the things you would like to do than to do everything only adequately. In intranet terms, small is beautiful. It is the flabby, undefined nature of many intranets that make them essentially unusable infor-mation wastelands (see Chapter 2). Many organisations define the success of their intranets by their coverage. It is better to define success at this stage by how *well* it is doing what it does, not how *much* it is doing. In the context of the process of revamping an existing intranet, the information needs assessment process can be compared with the existing intranet and a more realistic content-map drafted.

Step 4: Organising content areas and producing a content-map

The information needs assessment process will provide you with the raw material to begin identifying content areas and the relationships between them. The setting of objectives within the context of a wider information policy will enable you to focus those content areas on achievable goals.

The selection of content areas and the drafting of a content-map will form the content management structure of your intranet. Content management structures are discussed in Chapter 4, which should be read in conjunction with this stage. It is important that the content management structure, and by extension the content areas themselves, reflects the structure of your organisation. For example, content areas should be defined with existing demarcations of responsibilities in mind. Not only is this easier to manage, it underpins the future management of those content areas with recognisable frameworks. In other words, issues relating to competition over the ownership of information can be avoided by making sure that content areas reflect existing responsibilities (see Chapter 3).

At this stage, content that falls within the responsibility of several groups should be identified and ring-fenced for special consideration. For example, staff skills information collated on a departmental basis might form the foundation for a new interdepartmental resource. These ring-fenced resources are discussed under step 9.

When revamping an existing intranet, the process of selecting content areas may require renegotiation between existing content creators. This renegotiation may proceed smoothly if content creators are keen to offload responsibility for failing areas of content, or it may be contentious. Either way, the negotiating tools to be relied upon are the information policy, the stated objectives of the intranet and the result of the information needs assessment, all established at earlier stages.

Content creators who are worried about losing control of content in which they have a vested interest, for example the skills of members of their department, can be involved at a later stage in the design and in the management of central core resources. This is again discussed further under step 9.

In setting out content areas it is important to restrict the scope of the intranet as far as possible. A small intranet with core, relevant information will be more useful and therefore more successful than an intranet that attempts to be comprehensive. Set out what you can do well, and do it well, do not try to do everything. All content areas that you identify should contain either everyday information that has a role in the organisation's processes, or information that may be less frequently needed but which is nevertheless critical. Examples may include contact information, policy documents and procedures manuals. All your content areas should be justified by the strategic objectives set out in step 2. If the strategic objectives do not justify the content area, then it does not belong on the intranet.

If you are revamping an existing intranet, selecting content areas may involve removing large parts of the existing content or relegating content to an archive. It may also involve shifting content between content areas. Both of these processes may involve negotiation with existing content creators. It is important to involve content creators in the entire process rather than dictating terms. A dialogue is better than a monologue. Nevertheless, intranets designed by committee will fail (by extension of the argument in Chapter 3), and ultimately the objectives, information needs assessment and broader information policy must be relied on to justify decisions.

At this stage you should clearly identify which content areas fulfil each aspect of your objectives. For example, content that has a communicative function should be distinguished from content that has an informational function. Where two content areas as defined by your objectives fall within the broader organisational structure of a single group of people, for example a department, they should be separated and treated as distinct content areas at this stage. In other words, you should not define a content area for a department that will fulfil two objectives; you should define two content areas, each fulfilling a single objective. Avoiding confusing objectives in individual content areas will enable you to define much more precisely their role on the intranet.

A content-map should be created showing not only all the content areas on your planned intranet, including those centrally managed resources, but also what objective each fulfils. This content-map will form the backbone content management structure of your intranet – the way in which the intranet is structurally divided into sites, subsites and individual pages. It is not necessary at this stage to go down to the level of individual pages, as long as you can identify within the context of your strategic objectives what each content area is intended to achieve. This content-map should form the organisation-orientated navigation structure, and form the basis of your organisation-orientated taxonomy, as set out in step 7. At the end of the process it should broadly reflect the management structure of the organisation you are working within. This is discussed further in Chapter 4.

Archives and special collections should be defined in parallel with the content-map of the visible intranet. The content-map of the visible intranet should be as small as possible – relegate to special collections or archives anything that can be. If in doubt, leave it out.

Step 5: Identifying teams

At this stage it is necessary to identify precisely who is responsible for what. Where an existing intranet is being revamped, the choice of teams may be dictated by established practice. Although not ideal, it is better to work with existing structures than to alienate those who are already involved.

Intranets should be managed on a team basis. IT skills are not enough in themselves to make intranets work, nor are communications, information or people management skills. Intranets are organisation-wide tools, and should be managed in a cross-departmental way. Intranet management teams should reflect the four management perspectives discussed at the beginning of this chapter. In other words, each member of an intranet management team should be responsible for liaising with content creators, for information management and architecture, for communicating the role of the intranet or for the underlying IT infrastructure. Several of these individual management roles may be combined in one individual. Intranet management teams should be small, consisting of at most three or four people. It is likely that the intranet management team will suggest itself during the previous four stages. When revamping an existing intranet, parts of that team or an entire team may already be in place. In these circumstances, selecting teams is less important than delineating responsibilities.

For each content area, a manager must also be identified. It is preferable to separate content-area management responsibilities from content creation responsibilities, and to use the existing management structure of the organisation. For example, managers of existing departments should be given additional responsibility to manage content areas that fall under those departments. Where there has been a separation of content on the basis of the strategic objectives of the intranet, content-area managers may find themselves in the position of managing more than one area.

For each content area, the content creator also needs to be identified. It is preferable that where there are multiple content areas under the responsibility of a single content-area manager, different content creators are responsible for each of those areas. This will avoid introducing confusion into the objective of each area by merging responsibilities. Content creators may find themselves in the position of producing content for a number of content areas under different content-area managers. In these circumstances, it is better that the objectives of these areas fall under the same broad categories. For example, it is better that one content creator is responsible for several communication-orientated content areas, than for one communications area, one informational area and one knowledge management area.

Content creators should be responsible for the content areas they work in. Any content that is produced by other people should be mediated through them. At this stage, content-area managers and creators can set about the task of identifying and planning content. The selection of content creators and content-area managers may introduce training needs issues, especially where an intranet is being implemented for the first time. Training should only take place once the policies and procedures for managing the intranet are in place, and should use those policies and procedures as its foundation.

Step 6: Design, style and policy

Step 6 is to design the visual appearance of the intranet, write style guides and create policies relating to archiving, approving content, publicising content and any other issues related to the day-to-day management of the intranet. The intranet team must manage this entire process in liaison with content creators.

The visual design of an intranet is possibly the least important aspect from an information management perspective, but is often the most worried over. Providing guidelines for creating usable websites are followed, the details of the actual visual design, such as the colour scheme, typefaces used or layout of the page, are of little consequence. It is likely that the visual design will change over time, and providing that the content is prepared in the correct way, it should be possible to change from one visual design to another overnight. For this reason, consultation over visual design should be as wide as is practicable. The visual design should be decided with reference to the many guidebooks on web design available, some of which are listed in the appendix at the end of the book. Providing the visual design is intelligently and thoughtfully put together, its impact on the continued management of the intranet should be minimal.

Style guides are more important, and should define not just the appearance of pages (where that is not managed by the use of a content management system) but also the manner in which content is produced. Particular attention should be paid to consistency in titling, metadata and file management. These will impact on the future management of your intranet, especially if a full content management system has not been implemented. Archiving policies should also be set. Your aim is to make the visible intranet as small as possible. You should force expiration review dates across all content, and enforce their management.

At this stage you should also generate a policy workflow procedure for intranet content – all the stages that content needs to progress through before it is published. At the very least this should include both content area manager and intranet management team approval, and must define qualities that need to be included in content before it is published – for example expiration dates or meta-tags. For an existing intranet, establishing workflow procedures may require overturning existing procedures for creating content, and this may cause friction with content creators. For example, content creators who are used to publishing exactly what they want may find the new workflow routine overly bureaucratic. See Chapter 6 for more information on content workflow.

Step 7: Information architecture

The next stage is to set out the broad information architecture. This involves defining the various forms of navigation structure described in Chapter 4. The content management structure should be formed from the content-map set out in step 4. This content management structure will form a fixed structure to understand your intranet from a management perspective.

The content described under each content area can then be reorganised in relation to its format. For example, a second content-map may be drafted that shows the types of content available, be that procedures manuals, policies, forms, letters, etc. This second content-map can be used to formulise an information-orientated navigation design. The two content-maps can be combined to give a map that describes content not only in terms of management responsibilities but also in terms of its form. These two maps should be as comprehensive as possible, and if you are able at this stage to extend their coverage down to individual pages, then you should do so.

A third, process-orientated map should be drawn up. This will rely on the findings of your information needs assessment. By assessing information needs you will uncover the processes within the organisation in which information plays a part. This map can be used to design a process-orientated navigation scheme. At this stage the various content maps will be fixed, but as soon as your intranet is in operation as a live information tool, the content-maps covering your intranet will shift fluidly in real time, and it may not be possible again to draw up precise maps of current content again.

Once these navigation structures have been prepared, precise navigation terms reflecting the content they map must be selected. These terms should be rooted in the vocabularies of the organisation. For example, where specific technical terms are commonly used within the organisation, they should be reflected in the choice of terms used in navigation design.

At this stage, for an HTML-implemented intranet, you can begin the implementation of the navigation alternatives. However, should you choose a metadata approach to producing navigation aids dynamically, as is recommended, these content maps must be turned into metadata. Each of these maps will represent one facet either in a traditional thesaurus or in a spiral classification scheme. Each of the subordinate levels in your information map will represent subordinate terms within those facets. Continuing this process through all the structural levels of each of your content-maps will give you a metadata taxonomy that defines each page in relation to who is responsible for it, what kind of data it is, and what business processes it is involved in, in other words in terms of the content management structure, information-orientated structure and process-orientated structure. This should be combined with such metadata elements as are needed to control the content creation work-flow process – for example authorship, authorisation, pro-duction dates and expiry dates. For more on this, see the content workflow set out in Figure 5.1 at the end of this chapter.

With a traditional thesaurus approach, the relationship between these elements will largely be locked at this stage. It will be possible to introduce new terms and new classifi-cations, but these new classifications must fit inside an existing structure. With a spiral classification approach, this structure acts as a starting point for the ongoing classifica-tion of information and over time the structural relation-ships of each element will change.

With either approach, metadata must be combined with the database back-end in order to generate dynamic naviga-tion aids. From the end users' perspective, the results will appear indistinguishable from manually coded navigation schemes. Responsibility for meta-tagging content and main-taining the taxonomy must be ascribed at this stage. With thesaurus classification techniques, maintenance of the taxon-omy and possibly the meta-tagging should be centrally controlled, and this can be incorporated in the content workflow, becoming the last stage of that process after content creation and approval. With spiral classification techniques, it is preferable that content creators are given more control over selecting meta-tags, and for creating new classification terms, but a review of this work should be incorporated into the content workflow. Responsibility for this review should lie with the intranet manager controlling the information architecture of the intranet, but responsi-bility for combining the metadata with the database to gen-erate dynamic content may naturally lie with the manager responsible for IT issues.

Step 8: Selecting pathway editors

This step should be skipped if a database solution is being implemented. In such circumstances the role of pathway editor will be made redundant by the descriptive metadata.

However, where the intranet is managed traditionally, pathway editors are critical to maintaining the process hierarchies. Pathway editors should be independent of content, and should not be involved in content creation. They should be selected on the basis of their expertise within the processes for which they take responsibility, and on the basis of any existing responsibilities for managing those processes. For example, an editor responsible for a staff induction pathway may be found in someone with existing responsibility for staff induction.

The pathway editors will be responsible for surveying existing content on an intranet and for creating pages repackaging that content around the processes for which they are responsible. This may involve as little as producing pages of links to different content areas, or it could involve repackaging existing content within new contexts, where the technological infrastructure allows. The role of the pathway editor is dependent on the effectiveness of the style guides and policies set out in step 6. Without these being consistently applied, it will not be possible to repackage existing content in such a way as to make it appear that it belongs in its new context. The pathway editors should be given responsibility for ensuring that their pathways are current and exhaustive. Because pathway editors have no role in the creation of the content they repackage, they will be better able to keep an overview of the entire content landscape.

Step 9: Centrally managed resources

By now, your intranet should be beginning to approach its final shape. The next stage is to prepare the central resources ring-fenced in step 4. These may include such resources as staff skills directories, useful links collections or other content that may be usefully implemented *across* content areas. Centrally managed resources should be produced such that the content can be repackaged for use within content areas or pathways. For example, a staff skills directory should be implemented in such a way that individual content areas are able to draw information about staff directly from that directory, and present it as if it were a part of their content. This will require the use of a database.

Responsibility for *managing* these central resources can either be maintained within the intranet management team or delegated to individuals outside of that team. However, content creators should have a role in *maintaining* the information. For example, with a skills directory content creators are likely to have greater understanding of the skills resources related to their content areas than the management team, and they should therefore have a role in identifying and updating this information.

When preparing central resources, utilise existing responsibilities within the organisation. For example, whoever is responsible for maintaining phone lists should take responsibility for maintaining an intranet phone list, and where that list is combined with other types of information such as human resources information, responsibilities should be *divided* between individuals who have existing responsibilities. These should be collaborative resources updated from many sources but managed centrally – a mirror of the intranet itself.

Designing central resources will involve assessing the different needs that individuals or groups have of that resource, as discussed in Chapter 3. When revamping an existing intranet or changing the means by which information is delivered (e.g. from a paper telephone directory to an intranet directory) negotiation with the parties involved may be required. In such circumstances, it is preferable to liaise between groups until agreement is reached than to bring groups together to reach an agreement. Groups within an organisation are more likely to find common ground if they are not given cause to compete.

Step 10: Piloting and previewing

When revamping an existing intranet, it may be preferable to develop the new content and structure 'live' rather than in parallel with the existing content and structure. In such circumstances, the intranet will evolve rather than be relaunched, and there may be no need to pilot it. However, when developing a new intranet, or redeveloping in parallel with the existing provision, piloting of the new resource is essential. Piloting should be an evolving process, beginning as early as possible in the design stage. Feedback from pilots can usefully be incorporated into the other stages of design set out above.

Piloting teams should be selected to include as many interested parties as possible – content creators, management and pathway editors. Individuals with specific roles in relation to the intranet should be grouped together into separate pilot groups to avoid the prejudices of one set of individuals influencing the outcome of the piloting process. Pilots must also include people who have had no involvement with the development of the intranet. Feedback from piloting can be incorporated into the navigation design the visual design and other elements of the intranet. However, it is important not to be taken off track by the piloting process – it will not be possible to suit everybody's tastes. Concentrate on real issues rather than foibles.

It is also important to identify missing areas of content. However, be realistic about what you can achieve within the strategic objectives and information policy. It will not be possible to develop every item on a wish list, nor desirable or efficient to do so. The piloting process should be used to highlight serious flaws or omissions, not to redesign the intranet by committee.

Step 11: Rolling out the intranet

The last stage is launching the new or redesigned intranet. This can either be achieved across an organisation at one time or in a series of stages, depending on what is most appropriate (and depending on the physical structure in place, as outlined in Chapter 4).

There is insufficient space here to go into detail about launching an intranet, but some of the issues that you should take into account include: communicating with staff and forewarning them of what is going to happen, offering training, incorporating a feedback mechanism and marketing the launch. Try to avoid obvious times of high workload for your launch – people will be less receptive on a Monday morning than on a Thursday morning, and people will be less receptive if their budget deadline is approaching than if it has just passed. Try not to antagonise people by presenting them with a new system to learn at precisely the time they are most busy.

The launch is the first opportunity to persuade users of the usefulness of the intranet, and the first step in a process of ongoing maintenance and updating. However, intranets are not made or broken by their launch, but in their continued maintenance. This will be the subject of the next chapter.

Implementing intranets flowchart

Figure 5.1   Implementing intranets flowchart

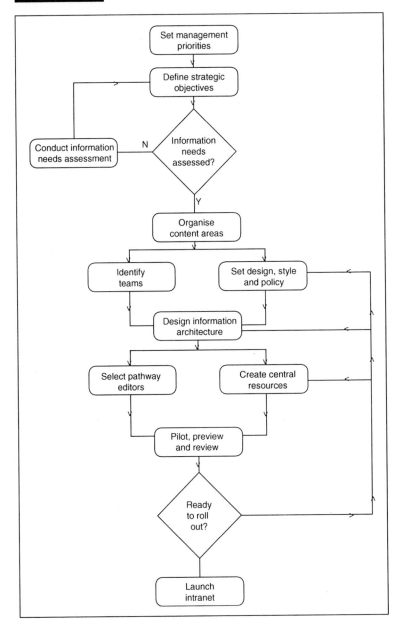

6

A step-by-step guide to managing intranets

Aims

This chapter follows on from the last. If your intranet is not modelled on the basis of Chapter 5, this chapter will still be a useful guide to managing your intranet, but you may find that some of the advice needs to be adapted to suit your needs.

The chapter outlines in a series of 14 steps the process of managing an intranet. The approach concentrates on the management processes rather than the management of specific technological solutions. The chapter draws directly on material discussed in other parts of the book, and it is recommended that you read earlier parts before reviewing this chapter. There is insufficient space in a book such as this to outline each stage with sufficient detail to allow this step-by-step guide to stand in isolation from previous chapters.

The 14 steps in the management of intranets outlined below are:

Step 1: Intranet management styles

Step 2: Intranet management cycle

Step 3: Identifying needs

Step 4: Content creation process

Step 5: Content approval process

Step 6:   Content deployment process

Step 7:   Content review process

Step 8:   Content deletion and archival process

Step 9:   Managing people

Step 10:   Managing central resources

Step 11:   Managing pathway editors

Step 12:   Managing user feedback

Step 13:   Managing infrastructure

Step 14:   Managing hierarchies.

Step 1: Intranet management styles

Intranet management styles were introduced in the previous chapter. The background for the discussion on management styles can be found in Part 1 of this book. The key contention throughout this text is that intranets fail, in their management as well as their design, by paying insufficient attention to the needs of people and the way in which people react to complex information resources in real-world settings.

Intranets can be managed on a number of levels. First, the IT infrastructure can be managed: the networks, servers and software maintained, and the traffic flows across the network managed. This forms an important prerequisite to delivering intranets: without the IT infrastructure, the intranet cannot function. The next level is that of communications: not just the way the intranet is discussed and promoted within an organisation, but also the communications media it is intended to replace, be that printed material for manuals, letters and forms, or face-to-face communication for skills directories etc. The next level of management is the design and maintenance of the information architecture. The final level is managing people: managing the individuals who play a part in creating or maintaining the resource, and also the individuals who use the resource. If an intranet is to continue to evolve and develop, fluidity must be maintained between these priorities.

For intranet managers, technological issues often take priority. The intranet is seen as a technological solution to information or communications needs. The next priority will usually be communication issues: *how can we use this intranet to save money and increase efficiency?* Informational concerns will usually form the third priority: *how are we going to make this resource usable?* Sometimes, information architecture will be neglected in favour of technological solutions. The lowest priority is frequently managing the people involved in creating and using the resource. One frequent assumption is that once the infrastructure is put in place, content creators can be left to work within that existing framework.

This book argues that managing intranets is principally a process of managing the expectations of those involved in creating and using intranets. Secondarily it is a process of managing information architectures. Only if information needs, expectations and structures are aligned can a realistic approach to managing those communications media that the intranet will replace be adopted. The lowest priority should be the technological approach taken to implement the resource. Technological solutions can vary and a range of solutions can be adopted for any given problem. Intranets, however, should be problem-led rather than solution-led. They should provide solutions to identifiable problems in information delivery within organisations. This means concentrating on what people do rather than how they do it, not only in the creation of content but also in their day-to-day use of information.

Intranets should be managed as a fluid resource rather than as the fixed or slowly evolving collections with which information professionals are more familiar. This means relinquishing precise control over the content that makes up that collection, and prioritising the needs of individuals, as mediated by content creators. This depends on content creators and content-area managers being able to reflect in their own experience and expertise the changing information needs of the groups that they are serving within the organisation. Information should bubble up through the management structures of intranets rather than rain down from above.

By adopting the hierarchy of management priorities focused firstly around people, then around information architecture, then around communications function and only lastly around technological solutions, the shifting information needs of individuals and groups within an organisation can be met. This can be represented in an inverse of the pyramid described in Chapter 3 (Figure 6.1).

Figure 6.1   Management priorities

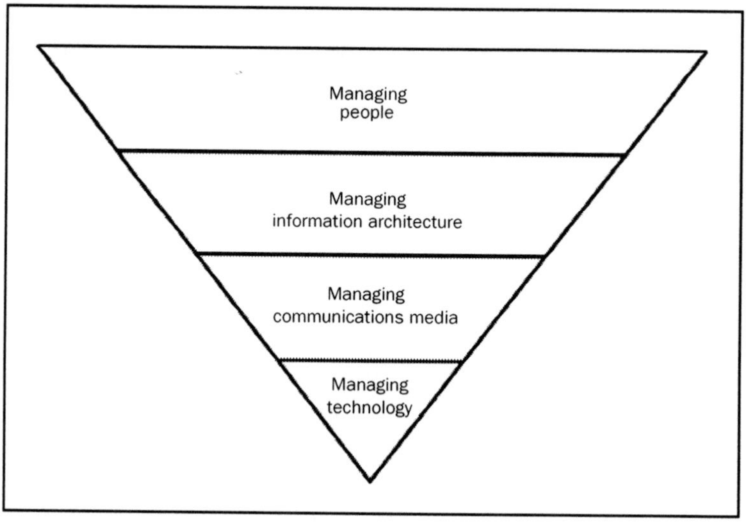

Step 2: Intranet management cycle

As we have seen above, managing intranets is not primarily about managing technology, or indeed information, but rather managing the processes that people exploit to create and use content. Steps 4 to 8 in this step-by-step guide outline the different processes involved, but we must first identify the cycle of management involved.

Intranets are made up of individual pieces of content. Depending on the precise technological infrastructure of your intranet, it may be possible to identify discrete pages within your intranet: intranets consisting of traditional HTML files resolve to discussion of individual pages whereas database-driven content management systems perhaps do not. For the purposes of discussion, however, the single, indivisible unit of information involved in intranet management can be regarded as the page. The intranet page will go through a life cycle similar to that shown in Figure 6.2, from identification of a need, creation of the page, approval of the page, deployment of the page, use of the page and finally to a review of the page; it is then either deleted, archived, updated or left in place. At each stage in this cycle there are issues that are discussed in detail in the steps below.

This life cycle of the individual page of content is the foundation of the management of intranets. Everything that happens to intranet content should be triggered by the stages within this cycle. For example, the delegation of responsibility for creating content is triggered by an identification of need, and the updating of navigational hierarchies is triggered by the deployment of content. As far as possible, the processes that depend on the life cycles of individual pages should be triggered automatically, whether this is implemented as a technological solution or as a managerial-process solution.

Figure 6.2 Content life cycle

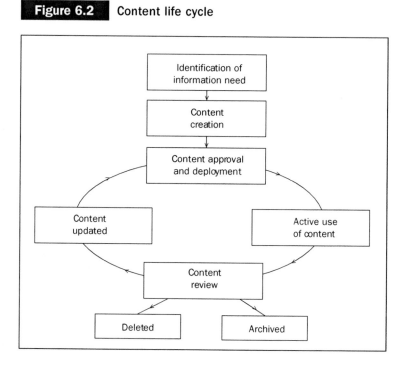

Intranets usually fail because of a failure to master this management cycle fully. An intranet where this cycle is not properly managed will inevitably deteriorate over time. It will become an unwieldy information wasteland and the navigation will become ineffective. In particular, the importance of deleting and archiving old information should not be underestimated.

Step 3: Identifying needs

The first stage in this life cycle is that of identifying an information need. This responsibility should lie with the content creators or content-area managers themselves, who if appropriately selected should have the real expertise in the information needs for any given content area. This relies on successfully dealing with information ownership issues at the implementation stage, as covered in Chapter 5.

Content creators and area managers should be encouraged to automate the identification of needs as far as possible. This may come in the form of regular consultation with users, e-mail bulletins from external information sources such as governmental or legislative information, or other similar triggers. The formulating of content-review policies discussed in Step 7 can also act as an automated trigger to content creation.

This automated triggering will not always be possible, and there will be a requirement to rely on the subject-expertise of individual content creators and area managers. Content creators and managers will see their role primarily as servicing the needs of the group they represent (see Chapter 3). However, the needs that they identify in the course of their work will not necessarily be exclusively those of the group they represent. It is therefore important that processes are established to allow content creators to pass upwards any identified information needs they do not feel are covered by the remit for their own content area, to enable reallocation of responsibility for fulfilling that need.

Communication between content creators and the groups they represent should be encouraged. This will be reinforced partly by the imposition of content-area managers with wider managerial responsibility for communities of interest, such as departments. Part of that communication can be conducted via the intranet itself, in the form of feedback mechanisms such as e-mail links. However, intranet-based methods of obtaining feedback and input from user groups will not in themselves suffice, as only those using the resource and whose needs are therefore already at least partly served will be able to participate.

In their initial identification of a need for new content, creators should be able to refer to guidance on the selection of content. In particular, creators should be required to identify which of the strategic objectives the content is intended to fulfil, allowing for the possibility that it fulfils some other need that can feed back into a review of objectives. This initial assessment of information need should be conducted with reference to the wider information policy, while acknowledging that the intranet may not be the best means of fulfilling the need. The assessment may take the form of a decision-tree or flowchart, however the degree of commitment required by the pre-production assessment may inhibit content creation, and wherever possible creators should be required to identify characteristics of information needs leaving the decisions regarding deployment of resources for fulfilling those needs at the management level.

Step 4: Content creation process

Content creation should include measures to ensure the inclusion of metadata that at the very least identify who is responsible for information, and when it is due to be reviewed. This should form a part of the content workflow, which can either be controlled by the use of a content management system or through managerial processes. Content workflows should also include approval procedures. A degree of automation may be incorporated into this process so that it becomes impossible for content to go from creation to deployment without fulfilling the requirements made of it.

At the point of creation, content will be 'owned' by its creators. Until this point, there need be no managerial control over the creation of content, other than the policy and style guides that define its appropriateness.

Step 5: Content approval process

Once a page of content has been created, it should enter a holding stage awaiting approval. Time is a critical factor in this process, especially for content that has a communicative function. For this reason, prioritisation of the approval of content should be based on the objective of the content as defined by the content creators within the framework of the strategic objectives of the intranet. In other words, if the strategic objectives of the intranet prioritise the communicative function over the informative function, then approval of content with a communicative function should be prioritised over that of content with an informative function. This will enable approval procedures to follow the form of content and prevent the objectives of the intranet from becoming obstructed by approval procedures.

Approval must occur as quickly as possible. This will necessitate managing workloads and priorities. Those involved in approving content must view that role as a priority. Approval should occur at as low a management level as is possible, with responsibility passed up to more senior management levels when difficulties arise. Procedures for covering the approval work during times of staff sickness or holiday should be put in place. It is vital that the approval stage does not become a bottleneck in the process of creating and deploying content. Should it become so, it will not only impact on the ability of the intranet to meet its objectives, but also deter content creators from producing good quality content.

The approval process should be conducted with reference to the specific coverage of the content area for which it is intended, in light of the coverage of other content areas, and content approved on the basis that:

- it is suitable within the framework of strategic objectives;
- it includes all required elements such as horizontal hyperlinks or metadata;
- it meets guidelines for style or format, including any policies for specific file formats.

The approval process should be properly formulated and transparent. Fast-track procedures may be appropriate for content that has had some degree of prior approval, for example updated rather than new content, or for particularly trusted content creators. The latter may be formalised in policy, with specified levels of content creator permissions.

Where content cannot be approved, content creators should be kept informed. Specific reasons for failure of approval should be given. Any delays in the approval process, caused, for example, by passing the content up the management chain, should be communicated to the content creators. The aim should be that all content will be approved, because all content creators will be sufficiently aware of the expectation made of that content prior to passing it on. In circumstances where content from specific departments or individuals is regularly refused approval, the procedures involved may need recommunicating or renegotiating.

Step 6: Content deployment process

Once approved, content should be deployed with as little delay as possible. This may depend on the IT infrastructure of your intranet. For example, with a distributed intranet it may only be possible to make new information available overnight or on a weekly basis. This will in part determine the type of content available on an intranet. See Chapter 4 for more information on this subject.

Making content available consists of several discrete steps:

1. The new content must be integrated into the structure of the intranet. In an HTML file-based intranet, this may be determined initially by the content areas within which content creators work. However, new content will also need to be incorporated within information- and process-orientated navigation schemes. This may include informing pathway editors of new content as it becomes available. With a database implementation, the location of new content within the existing taxonomies should be generated from the metadata classification terms allocated.

2. The new content needs to be publicised. There are three levels of publicity available: content-area wide, intranet wide and organisational wide. Content-area-wide publicity might involve content creators summarising new or updated content within their content area for the users of that content area. This will have the advantage of reaching the users who are most likely to need informing of the new content and may be a prerequisite to the deployment of new or updated information. Intranet-wide publicity might include informing users of new information added to the intranet via the main intranet home page. This should not be used for every addition or update to the intranet, but only for those updates of sufficient value to a wider audience. The intranet-wide update list should therefore be managed as a central resource (see Chapter 5). Organisation-wide publicity might include using media

other than the intranet, such as e-mail. Such publicity should be reserved for business-critical communications and updates or for significant redevelopments of content areas.

3. The final step in deploying new or updated content is encouraging the creation of horizontal hyperlinks between content areas, by informing content creators and area managers of recent additions and updates to the intranet. This need not happen concurrently with deployment: a weekly digest of all the additions and updates sent out to content creators may suffice. Information about updates should be targeted to those content creators who are most likely to find it relevant, and if using a database approach this can be achieved by comparing the metadata for the new content with that for existing content to establish likely related fields of interest. This process may be automated.

Step 7: Content review process

All information published on an intranet should have metadata indicating an explicit review date, review period and a suggested review action added at the production stage. For example, a news item may have a review period of one month, a review date therefore automatically generated for one month after its deployment and a suggested review action of deletion. At the end of that month, the news item can be identified as requiring review, fed into a review process and probably (although not certainly) deleted. Other actions may include: *update, ongoing review* and *archive*. Review periods should be implemented as fixed periods, i.e. monthly, bimonthly, quarterly, half-yearly and yearly.

Using a content management system approach, it should be straightforward to generate automatic lists of content that requires reviewing. With an HTML file approach, this is still relatively simple to achieve by using the search engine to index the metadata and pull out content based on its review date, although it may not be possible to automate that process.

The intranet management team should initially review content that has reached its review date. This may lead to its deletion, archiving or return to the content creator for updating. Information that is scheduled for deletion or archiving should nevertheless be returned to the content creator as a matter of courtesy, and also for final assessment. It is likely to be more practical with an HTML file approach to allow content creators to delete their own outdated content, provided this is a managed process.

Content scheduled for archiving can then be archived. Content set for updating, or for reviewing of its continued relevance, must enter a holding stage until such time as the content creator has confirmed the update or continued relevance, in which case the metadata should be automatically updated. It is recommended that content stay in this holding stage for only a short period of time before being suspended. As far as possible, this process should be automated.

Step 8: Deleting and archiving content

All hyperlinks pointing at deleted material must be removed at the point that the material is deleted. It is recommended that the hyperlinks are initially suspended – the links removed but the labels left – and that content creators are then warned of the deletion of the material they have linked to so that they can edit linked content appropriately.

All hyperlinks to material that is due to be archived can be automatically amended. Some indication that the material is now archived should be added to the hyperlinks. Content creators whose material contains such links should be informed of the new status of the material, because the context of the material may alter the way in which they contextualise it.

Step 9: Managing people

Throughout the stages in the management of intranets described above, three things should be apparent:

1. The incorporation of triggers that automatically initiate events.

2. That these triggers follow on from the initial creation or updating of content and that everything that happens to the content of an intranet thereafter is dependent on the way in which that content is initially defined and classified.

3. That these management processes are all prefigured by the work of content creators, and involve day-to-day communication.

In this model content creators retain their control over content, and intranet managers facilitate the process of managing that information effectively.

This relies on effective communication. Reports should be generated for individual content creators on a regular basis, outlining which parts of their content require review, which parts are scheduled for archiving or deleting, which information to which they have linked has been deleted or archived, and what additional content there is available to which they may want to link. These reports can be generated manually, but it will be more efficient to generate them automatically using the same metadata that control the content creation and deployment process, namely: authorship details, classification, review date, review period and review action. Content creators should also be given information about the usage of their content area.

Although it is possible to instigate live reporting, it is better to produce reports on a periodic basis. The model above relies on events triggering action, and reports produced periodically should themselves trigger action in content creators. If they can rely on the scheduling of these reports, they will be able to plan their workload more effectively. Providing live reporting, although superficially more impressive, throws the onus for triggering action onto content creators. A fundamental shift in responsibility would be put in place by using live reporting, similar to that discussed for the communicative function of intranets in Chapter 2. Systems based on human memory are liable to human fallibility.

Content creators should be notified as reports are updated. This can be automated, using scheduled tasks, but this must be overseen to pick up any problems with the automatic scheduling. The easiest way to do this is to counter-notify the intranet managers as a part of the same process. Where an intranet has not been implemented using a database solution, reporting of this kind should still be possible using a combination of customised search engines and weblog usage analysis, although this may require more manual input.

Step 10: Managing central resources

The life cycle for central resources, phone lists, e-mail directories, useful links directories, etc., follows exactly the same pattern as that for normal content outlined above. The difference is that central resources are centrally managed but updated by distributed means. For example, with a skills database, content creators for content areas such as departmental sites may be given the responsibility of updating records for the employees within their department, but this is incorporated into a single resource combining the information from all departments. It is critical that that information is still gathered from content creators in a distributed way. Content creators will not rely on the central resource unless they are confident that they are able to share in its generation.

The key difference between central resources and other content is the amount of control the intranet managers impose on the format and function of the data involved. With standard intranet content, the content creators to a greater extent manage and control their own content, within the boundaries of guidelines and processes set out by the intranet managers. However, with centralised resources, content creators are adding information in a format defined centrally. This lack of ownership of the resource by content creators may create a reluctance to update the information. Therefore, greater control over the resource has to be maintained. Each record in a directory, for example, should incorporate elements of metadata that define who is responsible for updating it, and when it was last updated. In this way, the evolution of the resource can be tracked.

Where a resource is extendable, for example a useful links database, it is better to allow content creators, and perhaps also users, to *submit* suggestions for additions to the resource to the intranet team, rather than to make additions themselves. This should prevent any duplication of information. For resources that are not extendable, such as directories of staff, the structure of the database will itself prevent duplication of information.

Step 11: Managing pathway editors

The role of pathway editor, where an automated process-orientated taxonomy has not been implemented, falls somewhat outside the day-to-day processes of content management. Pathway editors should be kept informed of updates and additions to the intranet via the same means as content creators. In other words, they should receive the same reports about additions and deletions to the intranet, enabling them to act on the information.

Pathway editing is necessarily time-intensive and requires a greater breadth of understanding of the entire information field within a given process than does content creation. For this reason, pathway editors should be drawn from experts within any given process, and this expertise is their key asset in managing the currency of their pathways. However, pathway editors should also be encouraged to feed back into the content creation process where they see gaps in the information available to make up their process pathways.

Pathways should be treated as evolving resources, just like any other type of intranet content. A pathway will not stay current indefinitely, and should be subject to the same periodic review. Some pathways may undergo frequent change, and the pathway editors will consequently be active in their management of the pathway. Other pathways may require less day-to-day management, and as a result it is *more* important that they are brought under the periodic review process.

Step 12: Managing user feedback

The general pattern of usage for any individual piece of content on an intranet is that it will receive most hits as it is deployed and users become aware of it. This will decline to a stable level as long as the information remains useful. When it has gone beyond its useful life, usage will decline still further. If the page is updated, usage will again peak as the information is deployed. These patterns of usage can be used to promote individual pieces of content into the review stage if usage figures suggest that its useful life has passed.

However, uselessness is not the only reason for under-usage of intranet content. Information on the patterns of use can be used to ascertain blind-spots on the intranet – pages that should be under high demand but that are not. Causes of blind spots may include:

- the information being poorly demarcated;
- the information being in the wrong place;
- the information competing with another resource;
- the information being under-publicised.

Where blind spots are identified, they should be tackled. This may involve re-publicising the content, defining it more appropriately (altering the title, the metadata or the labels of the links leading to it, etc.) or investigating the usefulness of the competing resource.

Do not rely overly on usage logs to determine the useful-ness of information. Some information may only be used on a periodic basis but is still critical to the organisation or indi-viduals – it may only be required once a year and therefore appear to be unneeded for most of the time. Some informa-tion that is infrequently used may be critical on those occasions when it is. Undertake a qualitative assessment of content as well as a quantitative assessment of usage logs in determining the usefulness of content. However, where a resource continues to be underused despite all attempts to promote it, there will come a time when it will need to be accepted that the resource as provided simply does not fulfil user needs.

Usage logs are not the only way of receiving feedback from users, although they have the advantage of unobtrusiveness. Users will contact content creators and the intranet team from time to time with queries and complaints, and particular attention should be paid to what they say. Try to stay away from inundating users with questionnaires about the intranet, usefulness of the intranet, their use of the intranet and other kinds of direct research. Although these can be useful occasionally, they can also give the impression of an intranet that is always talking about itself, and that does not pay adequate attention to its actual place amid a range of communications and information media. This kind of direct assessment of user attitudes should be conducted from the perspective of a wider communications policy if possible.

Step 13: Managing infrastructure

IT breakdowns are ubiquitous to IT systems, and the way in which they are managed can greatly enhance the ultimate usability of those IT systems. The situation is complicated with a distributed intranet, as the IT managers may not themselves view the intranet on the same server as individual users. Therefore, breakdowns can occur without the knowledge of the intranet management team. If this occurs frequently enough, which may be as little as once a year, then people may come to distrust the reliability of the intranet. Rely on the network of content creators to keep you informed of localised IT breakdowns. Make it easy for them to feed you this information (perhaps by including panic buttons in your communications with them).

The intranet should become a 24-hour resource. Because of this, updating elements of the infrastructure – such as replacing servers – should be done without suspending the intranet. On a distributed intranet this can be achieved by redirecting users in one location to a server in another location while the work is being done. Large-scale changes to the intranet – for example the complete overhaul of existing provision – should ideally be performed in parallel with the existing resource, so that the existing service is maintained until such time as it is appropriate to switch to the new resource.

Step 14: Maintaining hierarchies

Although the process of maintaining the structural hierarchies should be integral to the process of creating content, it will still be periodically necessary to undertake a thorough review of the hierarchy. This will mean mapping out all the content of the intranet, and assessing the structural relationships between the different components. This is a lengthy and involved task. It is in this process that the skills of the information professional will be most tested.

Depending on the size of the intranet in question, this process should be undertaken at least every one to two years. It may not be practical to review the hierarchies more frequently than that, but in the case of a very small intranet, the more frequent the review the better. With the metadata approach, the process is one of assessing the relationships between the terms in the hierarchy. The suitability of the terms as applied to individual pages of content should be picked up as part of the content review.

7

Anticipating change

Aims

In this chapter we examine the role of change and continued development in the success of intranets. Some of this change may be anticipated, some unanticipated. We examine different types of change, including changes in personnel, organisational change and technological change. The final part of this chapter attempts to anticipate some of the changes that are likely to affect intranets in the future.

Managing for change

At no point in time will a successful intranet be a static resource. At no point in time will the information it houses become stable, or the navigation structures fixed. Intranets are media of change. Managing for change means managing information processes, rather than managing units of information as in traditional library collections. It means managing the processes by which pages are created, deployed, reviewed and eventually archived or deleted, rather than managing individual pages as we might manage books or journals. Change has therefore formed an undercurrent of this book.

Intranets fail when they are managed as information collections rather than as information processes. As statically managed intranets grow, they become unwieldy. The advice in this book is structured so as to encourage the management of intranets as resources in constant flux. That constant flux will make it impossible at any given time to know the precise shape of the resource and impossible to pin down the exact characteristics of the collection. Although the available information may be tracked, any content in preparation, being planned or yet to be recognised as an information need will go undefined – undefined but not unmanaged. By managing the entire process of creating, categorising, deploying and ultimately delivering information to the user, we are shaping the gradual evolution of the intranet.

But managing for change means more than just controlling an evolving resource: events and developments that are likely to influence the intranet in the future must also be anticipated. Some of these developments may involve people as they move on, both within an organisation and outside of it. Unless the transition between content creators is handled successfully, the loss of key content creators will undermine an intranet, casting what was useful information into decline. Some of those developments may be at an organisational level. Organisational priorities shift, new services are developed, the shape of the organisation changes and the content management structure of the intranet will need to change with it, because otherwise over time the intranet will increasingly less accurately reflect the organisation it serves. Occasionally, organisational change may be catastrophic as companies merge or are taken over. In such circumstances, the intranet may too be inflicted with total change.

Some of those developments may be on a technological level: new software and new approaches to solving traditional problems are developed. This technological development has to be incorporated into a management strategy in order to enable the intranet to continue to develop.

Intranet development is a process of evolution, not revolution. The pattern of relaunching an intranet every two or three years to take advantage of the latest technology or to restructure the information landscape of an intranet is neither good for the management of intranets nor for their users. Although, as discussed in Chapter 1, users can become so familiar with the architecture of an intranet that they stop seeing alternative pathways, presenting users with different interfaces every few years will alienate them from a resource that may have served their needs well. Change, whether it is on a personnel level, an organisational level or a technological level, should be a managed process.

Changes in personnel

People move on. Within organisations people are promoted to new jobs, taking on new responsibilities and challenges. People also move to new workplaces. For intranet managers, whether people move up or out is not a significant factor, but whether they move away from their involvement with the intranet is. When people move, either internally or externally, they take with them their skills and experience. A content creator who has spent years developing a content area may have no further involvement with it, and the intranet loses not only their skills in putting together content, but also their understanding of the users they serve and their knowledge of the available information resources.

Perhaps the most important people involved in the creation of an intranet are the content creators. They are the lifeblood of an intranet, generating new content and anticipating changing information demands within the content areas for which they are responsible. However, the content creator's role is also the most detached from the management of an intranet; they have least control over the strategic objectives of an intranet or the direction it develops in, and are likely to view their involvement with the intranet as a complex formed from their other roles within the organisation and membership of different groups. Change in content creators is difficult to manage: not only are they likely to move more frequently than other individuals involved with intranet projects – the intranet forms only part of their job – but when they move they tend to take with them important skills in assessment, collation and creation of content, together with knowledge of their userbase. These skills are not easy to replace.

Change in content creators must largely be managed within the context of the content areas they develop. As outlined in Chapter 5, the content-area manager should have wider responsibilities within the department or group reflected by the content area, and should be able to anticipate personnel change within this department or group. However, it is not sufficient to assume that this is the case. Content-area managers may well have an overview of the changes within their department or group, but the intranet content for which they are responsible is unlikely to be at the forefront of their mind, for reasons discussed in Chapter 3. It cannot therefore be assumed that content-area managers will appreciate the wider ramification of personnel changes within their department or group, or take the necessary steps to prepare for this change.

The necessary steps, including identifying people to take over the necessary content area, scheduling sufficient training and scheduling a hand-over period so that the skills of the content-creator can be passed on, may be formulated in policy or may be managed informally. Regardless, they must be actively managed. For this reason, communication must be maintained with the content-area managers.

Content-area managers themselves are likely to change with less frequency than content creators, because they will usually be more senior within an organisation. However, change in content-area managers may bring with it re-appraisal of the content area in question. Intranet managers should anticipate this, and prepare for the possibility by engaging with new content managers about the existing provision for which they are taking over responsibility as soon as possible. This may include providing more detailed usage statistics and discussing future strategy within the context of the strategic aims of the intranet. A change in content-area managers can be an opportunity to enhance the development of existing content areas.

Because of the expertise that defines the role of a pathway editor, finding replacements is likely to a more difficult process for the management team. Many pathway editors may be defined by their role within an organisation; for example, a pathway for staff induction may be developed within the context of a human resources role. In such circumstances, replacements for pathway editors may be sought within the department or role that the process pathway mirrors. However, some pathway editors may have less formally defined expertise, and their skills may be unique within an organisation. They may fulfil an informal or formal role as office expert, for example. In such circumstances where it is not possible to replace pathway editors, the specific pathways must be suspended after a period of time to avoid them becoming out of date and consequently misleading.

Changes to the intranet management team can bring about a more fundamental challenge to the future development of the intranet. Losses in management team members can cause not only a loss of their knowledge and expertise, which may be specific to the particular model adopted and therefore irreplaceable, but also introduce conflict into the team as new members bring with them their own outlooks and aspirations. Whichever way this is managed, there will need to be some level of reappraisal of the continued development and management of the intranet, not only on the management team level, but also on a senior management level, if the intranet is not to become locked in conflict between the way things used to be done and the way new team members want things to be done.

Personnel change should be seen as an opportunity. Changes in the people involved in the development of an intranet can lead to a loss of knowledge and expertise, but also bring re-evaluation of existing provision, new ideas and renewed enthusiasm.

Organisational change

Organisational change can occur on a strategic, a structural or a fundamental level. Strategic change may include a change in management priorities. Structural change may include the addition of departments or service lines, the loss of departments or service lines, the addition or loss of sites or offices, and other similar events. Fundamental or catastrophic change may include mergers, demergers and the various categories of takeovers. Any one of these three types of change may occur with more or less frequency, depending on the type of organisation. For example, in some sectors mergers are relatively frequent events, and in others the strategic direction of the organisation may change every two to three years. Whatever the precise circumstances, all will have a significant impact on the intranet.

A solid business model for the intranet, with good control of costs and quantifiable achievements, will do most to prepare an intranet for this form of change. In the case of strategic changes, it will help to prove the role of the intranet within the organisation.

Structural change may impact on the overall content coverage of the intranet. Intranets in sectors where this kind of change is frequent should have prepared procedures for developing new content areas and for removing old ones. These may include identifying individuals to take on the role of developing new content areas, which in the case of the introduction of new service lines or departments could mean the involvement of the intranet management team in the recruitment process. If an intranet is an important part of an organisation, it should be integral to the development of new services.

Fundamental change, particularly mergers and takeovers, may require two intranets to be merged, or two intranet models to be compared and one adopted. This is an involved process, and not one to be entered into lightly. The best advice is to be as prepared as possible. Most intranets are failing, and if yours is not one of these, it stands a good chance of coming through the process intact.

Technological change

Intranet technology is likely to change over time, to take advantage of increases in computing power and network capacities. However, some of the driving factors behind the technological advancement of intranets can be misplaced. Technology will not by itself solve the problem of failing intranets. Technology may not in itself aid users. However, although it is not inevitable that a managed intranet will become technologically more sophisticated over time – the publication model of Jennifer Stone Gonzales (1998) may serve the needs of a given organisation perfectly well – technological change is likely and must be managed.

The guiding principle behind assessing and implementing new technologies is not in evaluating what the technology can achieve but what existing problem it addresses. For example, video conferencing has a clear application, but before implementation it needs to be established whether there is an existing problem that it will address, such as quantifiable difficulties in teams meeting that causes bottlenecks in management processes. Without focusing technological advancement on identifiable problems, technology may introduce problems into the organisation without resolving any. For example, video conferencing may encourage employees to meet less often, leading to a breakdown in the coherence of teams and an entrenchment of individual interests. Introducing technology without clearly identifying need represents in microcosm exactly what has caused intranets to fail in so many organisations.

Change for users

Let us go back to the beginning: why do users behave irrationally? Or rather, why do we interpret user behaviour as irrational? Users are following information-seeking strategies that have been successful in similar resources elsewhere. The user is central to the success of an informational resource. When introducing change the user therefore has to be central to the process.

This means that change has to be addressed on the basis of what works for users, not what works for content creators, content-area managers, strategic managers, intranet managers or IT professionals. If something that works for the user is changed for the benefit of one of these other groups, then the explicit expectation that users have of their intranets will again become disappointed. The principle behind introducing change for users is that structural change should be initiated organically. For example, navigation schemes should not be redesigned overnight; a new navigation scheme must be introduced in a way that allows users to buy into the change – providing them with useful tools or capabilities to which previously they had no access.

In this context, content creators, content-area managers and strategic managers are also intranet users. This is not only because they also will use the intranet as an information resource, but also because when they are creating and managing content, they are using the resources and tools provided for that process. Change to these processes and tools must also be organic and focused on what added value is brought to the content creation process.

Information systems convergence

Information systems are converging. The file management system is becoming indistinguishable from the web resource. Browsers are becoming resource managers. Desktops are becoming web pages. In a few years time, there will be little distinction from the user's point of view between information held in a file on a shared network drive and information held on an intranet. Perhaps in a few years beyond that, whether information is held locally or externally will no longer be an issue in the manner of accessing that information, just as Tim Berners-Lee originally envisaged.

In the short term this will result in an increasing reliance on tools that promote *collaboration* over *communication*, tools that allow users to share files with built-in version-management protection. Over time, document management systems, content management systems and file management systems are likely to converge. This will mean that all the files on an organisation's network, be they work in progress, intranet content, word-processor files, database records, etc., will effectively form a seamless contour of information. The likelihood is that access will migrate towards rather than away from HTML models, towards the model of the intranet and away from the model of the file management system. It is likely in the future that every interaction a user makes with their computer will be in some way mediated by what we might call an intranet.

The invisible resource

Eventually, intranets will be replaced. Eventually, they will all fail. Eventually, this model of managing the delivery of certain classes of information via a discrete internal website with which users must electively engage in order to participate in the utilisation and development of an organisation's informational resources will pass. What will replace it is the invisible resource, seamlessly integrated with the users' work processes, and seamlessly integrated with their desktop, a fundamental part of the *use* of computers within organisations. When a user switches on their computer, they will be in an information environment rather than a computing environment – an information environment that manages not only the delivery of information to them but also the processing of that information by them. The intranet will not be a separate architecture. It will become a part of the architecture of network computing.

As information system convergence occurs, it will become more and more critical to distinguish between different types of information and application, to build structures within which that information and those applications can be managed, to build taxonomies, to classify, arrange, identify, select, shift and archive, to manage information rather than technology. The role of the information professional is growing and diversifying. The place for the information professional is developing. In the future, people who understand the management of information will become more and more in demand. And in this maelstrom of change, there is endless opportunity.

8

Conclusion

Why intranets fail ...

Why *do* intranets fail? This book has set out to answer that question. Each intranet is successful in the same way, but each is unique in its failure.

If there is one thing that I hope has become apparent, it is that intranets are *complex* systems. This complexity derives from the interactions of users, content creators and content managers, each with their own set of short-term or long-term priorities, causing eddies of self-generating feedback. In this, the intranet is a mirror of the organisation it serves, and it will reflect the internal politics of the organisation, the competition over resources, the squabbles and the collaboration. Managing an intranet is not a matter of managing a collection of information but of managing the processes by which people become informed.

... and how to fix them

The role of the information professional is changing more rapidly now that it has ever done. This reflects the ways in which information is used in society. Being informed was once a matter of access to information, access to collections, access to media and access to education. As we evolve from an industrial society to an information society, being informed is less and less a matter of access. Information itself, the physical collection, the writing, images and data that make up our information sources, becomes effectively cheaper by the day, easier to duplicate, process, pass on, disseminate, distribute and partake in. As information becomes cheaper, obtaining information becomes less important than processing it. The role of the information professional is migrating from the management of collections to the management of the processes by which people become informed.

Intranets thus need to be managed as systems that control that processing of information, that help to sift and filter that information, that help to deliver the right information to the right user at the right time and that help users become informed. This means that information on intranets must be managed not as a resource, or as a collection, but as a process.

This is not about technology, although technology can play a role. It is not about HTML or databases, or document and content management systems. It is not about networks and desktops. Making intranets work is a matter of identifying what information people need to do their jobs on a day-by-day basis, and delivering it to them. Deliver a killer-application on your intranet and people will use that application. Make your intranet a killer-application in itself and people will use the intranet. They may not care about the taxonomical structures, navigation aids or search tools. They may not distinguish when they are using the intranet and when not. They may not identify the intranet as the source of their being informed. But then why should they ... ?

A truly successful intranet allows the users to forget it is even there.

Appendix
Resource list

Aims

This appendix brings together a range of resources for the creation and design of intranets, which can act as further reading. It is divided into three sections:

- books about intranets
- books about web design
- Internet resources.

Books about intranets

There are two striking things about most of the books written on the subject of intranets. First, most were published in the late 1990s. Second, they exude the uncritical enthusiasm for the potential of intranets to which this book is in part intended to form a cautious coda. The list below is indicative rather than exhaustive.

Managing Your Internet and Intranet Services: The Information Professionals Guide to Strategy (Peter Griffiths, published by Facet Publishing, London, 2004). A useful overview of setting up and managing web services. Although only one chapter specifically deals with intranets, the book is helpful in its focus on information services and the role of information professionals. Although this is a new edition, it is strikingly similar to the previous edition published in 1997.

The 21st Century Intranet (Jennifer Stone Gonzales, published by Prentice Hall, 1998). A comprehensive book, covering all aspects of the development of an intranet.

Understanding Intranets: The Decision Maker's Guide to Technology (Tyson Greer, published by Microsoft Press, 1998). Concentrating on the potential of technology rather than on the management of intranets or issues associated with their use, this is nevertheless a useful book with a good step-by-step outline of the process of introducing an intranet.

Intranet Bible (Lynn M. Bremner, Anthony F. Iasi and Al Servati, published by Jamsa Press, 1997). From the *Bible* series. This attempts to be a comprehensive resource. It therefore tends to jump around from issue to issue, dealing with the absolute basics of using HTML alongside the role of intranets within organisations.

Collective Knowledge: Intranets, Productivity, and the Promise of the Knowledge Worker (Robert Marcus and Beverly Watters, Microsoft Press, 2002). Looks at intranets from the perspective of knowledge management.

Books about web design

There is something at once more critical and also more satisfying about many of the books written on general web design issues. They cover a lot of good ground, and anyone involved in designing for intranets will be able to take much good material from them. One slight word of caution: not all the advice that applies to websites applies to intranets; users of intranets have a different relationship with the resource, and therefore designing for intranets is a slightly different challenge.

Designing Web Usability: The Practice of Simplicity (Jakob Nielsen, published by New Riders, 2000). Jakob Nielsen is an evangelising guru of web design, and this book is full of good common sense that is easily accessible.

Don't Make Me Think: A Common Sense Approach to Web Usability (Steve Krug, published by Que, 2000). Another useful text on web usability.

World Wide Web resources

The resources below were current at the time of publication.

Web design

Useit.com (*http://www.useit.com*). Jakob Nielsen's usability website, full of useful information, not least the regular usability newsletter, *usit.com*.

The World Wide Web Consortium (*http://www.w3c.org*). The website of the World Wide Web Consortium (W3C for short), founded by Tim Berners-Lee. The site is a mine of information for issues related to the future of HTML and web standards.

The Intranet Journal (*http://www.intranetjournal.com*). An excellent resource containing articles and advice about all aspects of intranet development.

Keep It Simple Column (*http://www.digital-web.com/types/keep_it_simple/*). Peter-Paul Koch explores simplicity in web design in a series of columns.

(En)Visioning Interactive Stories (*http://www.wired.com/wired/archive/4.02/streetcred.html?pg=18*). Writing for hypertext, by Rob Swigart, published in *Wired* magazine.

Writing for Multimedia: A Guide (*http://home.earthlink.net/~atomic_rom/contents.htm*). By Michael Butzgy, a guide to writing for hypertext and multimedia.

Web Style Guide, 2nd edn (*http://www.webstyleguide.com/index.html?/sites/site_structure.html*). An excellent resource.

Information architecture

Ten Questions About Information Architecture (*http://builder.com.com/5100-31-5074224.html*). An introduction to information architecture, by Shel Kimen.

Budgeting

Intranet Cost Calculator (*http://intrack.com/intranet/costs/index.shtml*). From Intrack, a workable cost calculator in Excel Spreadsheet format.

Assessing Intranet Cost–Benefits (*http://www.fastrak-consulting.co.uk/tactix/Features/costbens/costbens.htm*).

Bibliography

August, V. (1999) 'Intranets fail to deliver business value', *TechWeb* (*http://www.techweb.com/wire/story/TWB19 990624S0011*).

Begbie, R. and Chudry, F. (2002) 'The intranet chaos matrix: a conceptual framework for designing an effective knowledge management intranet', *Journal of Database Marketing*, 9 (4): 325–38.

Bell, A. and Oxbrow, N. (2001) *Competing with Knowledge*. London: TFPL.

Berners-Lee, T. (1999) *Weaving the Web: The Origins and Future of the World Wide Web by Its Inventor*. London: Orion Business.

Bird, J. (1997) *The Reuters Guide to Good Information Strategy*. London: Reuters.

Blackmore, P. (1997) 'The development of an intranet within a college of further and higher education', *Aslib Proceedings*, 49 (4): 69–72.

Blackmore, P. (2001) *Intranets: A Guide to their Design, Implementation and Management*. London: ASLIB-ILI.

Bradford, S.C. (1934) 'Sources of information on specific subjects', *Engineering*, 137: 85–6.

Bremner, L.M., Iasi, A.F. and Serati, A. (1997) *Intranet Bible*. Las Vegas: Jamsa Press.

Brooks, T.A. (2004) 'The nature of meaning in the age of Google', *Information Research*, 9 (3): *http://informationr.net/ir/9-3/paper180.html*.

Coulson-Thomas, C.J. (2001) 'Managing intellectual capital', *Corporate Governance Handbook Newsletter*, June.

Coyne, K.P., Stover, A. and Nielsen, J. (2002) *Designing Usable Intranets*. Freemont, CA: Nielsen Norman Group.

Coyne, K.P., Goodwin, C. and Nielsen, J. (2003) *Intranet Design Annual 2003: Year's 10 Best Intranets*. Freemont, CA: Nielsen Norman Group.

Crystal, D. (2001) *Language and the Internet*. Cambridge: Cambridge University Press.

Currie, G. and Kerrin, M. (2004) 'The limits of a technological fix to knowledge management: epistemological, political and cultural issues in the case of intranet implementation', *Management Learning*, 35 (1): 9–29.

Duane, A. and Finnegan, P. (2003) 'Managing empowerment and control in an intranet environment', *Information Systems Journal*, 13: 133–58.

Duffy, D. (2001) 'Why do intranets fail?', *Darwin Magazine*, November: *http://www.darwinmag.com/real/110101/intranet.html*.

Edenius, M. and Borgerson, J. (2003) 'To manage knowledge by intranet', *Journal of Knowledge Management*, 7 (5): 124–36.

Fichended, J. (1997) 'Managing intranets to improve business processes', *ASLIB Proceedings*, 49 (4): 90–6.

Flood, G. (2001a) 'Is your intranet working?', *Information World Review*, 1 June.

Flood, G. (2001b) 'In step with your intranet?', *Information World Review*, 7 August.

Foucault, M. (2002a) *The Archaeology of Knowledge*. London: Routledge.

Foucault, M. (2002b) *The Order of Things*. London: Routledge.

Gibbs, C. (2001) 'Making the right E-content moves', *Information World Review*, 1 January: 18–21.

Gillies, J. and Cailliau, R. (2000) *How the Web Was Born*. Oxford: Oxford University Press.

Gonzalez, J.S. (1998) *The 21ˢᵗ Century Intranet*. Englewood Cliffs, NJ: Prentice Hall.

Greer, T. (1998) *Understanding Intranets: The Decision Maker's Guide to Technology*. Redmond, WA: Microsoft Press.

Griffiths, P. (2004) *Managing Your Internet & Intranet Services*, 2nd edn. London: Facet Publishing.

Gupta, J. and Wachter, R. (1997) 'The establishment and management of corporate intranets', *International Journal of Information Management*, 17 (6): 393–404.

Harvey, F. (2004) 'Bringing the outside in', *New Media Age*, February.

Information World Review (2001) 'Intranets failing', *Information World Review*, June: *http://www.iwr.co.uk/iwreview/1150481*.

Keynote Market Reports (2004) *Internet Usage in Business*. Keynote Market Reports.

Kosko, B. (1994) *Fuzzy Thinking: The New Science of Fuzzy Logic*. London: Flamingo.

Leer, A. (1999) *Masters of the Wired World: Cyberspace Speaks Out*. London: Pearson Education.

McLuhan, M. (2001) *Understanding Media*. London: Routledge.

Marcus, R. and Watters, B. (2002) *Collective Knowledge: Intranets, Productivity, and the Promise of the Knowledge Worker*. Redmond, WA: Microsoft Press.

Mercer (2003) *Intranets – Bad Design Wastes Company Time and Money*. London: Mercer Human Resource Consulting: *http://www.mercerhr.com/pressrelease/details .jhtml/dynamic/idContent/1091190;jsessionid=H3TT0U NG5ZEHOAAJAADQOCAKMZSI4I2C*.

Neal, D. (2002) 'Intranet success takes time', *IT Week*, 20 September: *www.itweek.co.uk/News/1134933*.

Nicholas, D. (1996) *Assessing Information Needs: Tools and Techniques*. London: ASLIB.

Nielsen, J. (2000) *Designing Web Usability: The Practice of Simplicity*. Indianapolis, IN: New Riders.

O'Flynn, S. (2000) 'Intranets and information values', *Vine*, 119: 17–18.

Popper, K. (2001) *Conjecture and Refutation*. London: Routledge.

Raber, D. (2003) *The Problem of Information: An Introduction to Information Science*. Lanham, MD: Scarecrow Press.

Raskin, J. (2000) *The Humane Interface: New Directions for Designing Interactive Systems*. Boston: Addison-Wesley.

Robertson, J. (2002a) 'What are the goals of a CMS', *Intranet Journal*, 3 September: *http://www.intranetjournal.com/articles/200209/it_09_03_02a.html*.

Robertson, J. (2002b) 'Sixteen steps to a renewed corporate intranet', *Intranet Journal*, 16 September: *http://www.intranetjournal.com/articles/200209/ij_09_16_02a.html*.

Robertson, J. (2002c) 'The value of web statistics', *Intranet Journal*, 22 February: *http://intranetjournal.com/articles/200202/km_02_27_02a.html*.

Rowley, J. (1998) *The Electronic Library*. London: Library Association.

Scheepers, R. (2003) 'Key roles in intranet implementation: the conquest and the aftermath', *Journal of Information Technology*, 18: 103–19.

Spink, A. (2004) 'Web search: emerging patterns', *Library Trends*, 52 (2): 299–306.

Tredinnick, L. (2001) 'Building an intranet content management strategy', *Vine*, 124: 20–6.

Wells, H.G. (1938) *World Brain*. London: Methuen.

White, M. (2002) *Benefits of Employee Online Communities*. Bristol: Sift: *http://www.sift.co.uk/practice/white-papers/mw_employee_communities.pdf*.

Wilkinson, L.J., Charleton, P. and Sice, P. (2000) 'Intranets and the learning organisation', *Vine*, 119: 11–16.

Wodehouse, Lord (1997) 'The intranet – the quiet (r)evolution', *ASLIB Proceedings*, 49 (12): 13–19.

van Vark, C. (2004) 'Search still sets the pace', *Revolution*, April: 84–5.

Zipf, G.K. (1949) *Human Behaviour and the Principle of Least Effort*. New York: Addison Wesley Press.

Index

Printed in the United States
71998LV00001B/47

9 781843 340935